AQA Certificate
Chemistry (iGCSE) Level 1/2

SCIENCE

Lawrie Ryan

Editor
Lawrie Ryan

REVISION GUIDE

Nelson Thornes

This edition published in 2013 by:
Nelson Thornes Ltd
Delta Place
27 Bath Road
CHELTENHAM
GL53 7TH
United Kingdom

13 14 15 16 17 / 10 9 8 7 6 5 4 3

A catalogue record for this book is available from the British Library

ISBN 978 1 4085 2116 8

Cover photograph: Image Source/Alamy

Page make-up by Wearset Ltd, Boldon, Tyne and Wear

Printed and bound in Spain by GraphyCems

Photo acknowledgements
C.1.2.1a Science Photos/Alamy; C.1.2.1b Science Photos/Alamy; C2.2.1 Bloomberg/Getty Images; C2.5.1 Science Photos/Alamy; C3.7.1a Laguna Design/Science Photo Library; C3.7.1b Pasieka/Science Photo Library; C4.3.1 Pete Will/iStockphoto; C5.2.2 Martyn F. Chillmaid/Science Photo Library; C5.3.2 Tony Craddock/Science Photo Library; C5.4.1 Andrew Lambert Photography/Science Photo Library; C6.5.3 Andrew Lambert Photography/Science Photo Library; C7.3.1 Fotolia; C7.4.2 Chris R. Sharp/Science Photo Library; C7.5.2 Alina Hart/iStockphoto; C7.5.2 Universal Images Group/Getty Images; C7.6.3 Martyn F. Chillmaid; C7.7.2 Pascal Goetgheluck/Science Photo Library; C7.8.2 Herreid/iStockphoto; C7.9.1 Denis Babenko/Fotolia; C9.2.2 Nyul/iStockphoto; C9.4.1 USDA; C9.4.3 Bloomberg via Getty Images; C10.1.3 Paul Rapson/Science Photo Library; C10.2.3 Kheng Guan Toh/Fotolia; C10.3.2 Inner Shadows/Fotolia; C10.4.2 Lya Cattel/iStockphoto; C10.4.3 CC Studio/Science Photo Library; C10.5.1 Ralph125/iStockphoto; C10.5.2 Josh Reynolds/AP/Press Association images; C11.2.1 Andrew Lambert Photography/Science Photo Library; C11.2.2 Studio Annika/iStockphoto; C11.3.1 Lawrence Migdale/Science Photo Library; C12.2.1 Martyn F. Chillmaid; C12.2.3 Fuse/Getty Images; C12.3.2 Martyn F. Chillmaid/Science Photo Library; C15.1.1 David Taylor/Science Photo Library; C15.2.1 Andrew Lambert Photography/Science Photo Library; C15.2.2 Charles D. Winters/Science Photo Library.

iGCSE Chemistry   Contents

Key points

At the start of each topic are the important points that you must remember.

🖩 Maths skills

This feature highlights the maths skills that you will need for your Science exams with short, visual explanations.

∞ links

Links will tell you where you can find more information about what you are learning and how different topics link up.

Welcome to AQA Level 1/2 Certificate in Chemistry

This book has been written for you by very experienced teachers and subject experts. It covers everything you need to revise for your exams and is packed full of features to help you achieve the very best that you can.

Key words are highlighted in the text. You can look them up in the glossary at the back of the book if you are not sure what they mean.

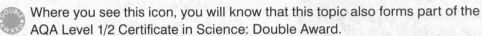 Where you see this icon, you will know that this topic also forms part of the AQA Level 1/2 Certificate in Science: Double Award.

➡ *These questions check that you understand what you're learning as you go along. The answers are all at the back of the book.*

Many diagrams are as important for you to learn as the text, so make sure you revise them carefully.

Study tip

Study tips give you important advice on things to remember and what to watch out for.

Practical

This feature helps you become familiar with key practicals. It may be a simple introduction, a reminder or the basis for a practical in the classroom.

At the end of each chapter you will find:

End of chapter questions

These questions will test you on what you have learned throughout the whole chapter, helping you to work out what you have understood and what you need to go back and revise.

And at the end of each unit you will find:

Examination-style questions

These questions are examples of the types of questions you will answer in your actual examination, so you can get lots of practice during your course.

You can find answers to the End of chapter and Examination-style questions at the back of the book.

C1.1

States of matter

Key points

- The three states of matter are solids, liquids and gases.
- The particles in a solid are packed closely together, fixed in their positions but vibrating constantly.
- The particles in a liquid are also close together but can slip and slide over each other in random motion.
- The particles in a gas have lots of space, on average, between them and zoom around randomly.

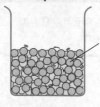

Solid
Particles vibrate

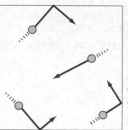

Liquid
Particles slip and slide over each other

Gas

Particles move very quickly in all directions; as the particles bash against the walls of the container, they exert a force that causes pressure

Figure 1 The particles in the three states of matter

Study tip

Some students make the mistake of thinking that the particles in a solid do not move, as solids cannot flow. However, the particles in a solid are constantly vibrating about their fixed positions.

- We can classify the majority of substances as **solids**, **liquids** or **gases**. These are called the three **states of matter**.
- To explain the properties of solids, liquids and gases we use the kinetic theory of matter. It is based on the fact that all matter is made up of tiny particles and describes:
  – the movement of the particles, and
  – the average distance between particles in each state of matter.

▸ **1** *In which state of matter can particles move around most freely?*

- Look at the changes of state that occur when water is heated and cooled:

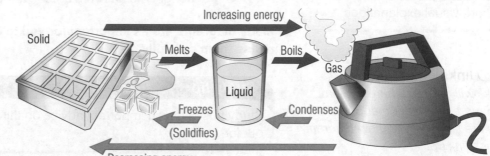

Figure 2 The changes of state in water

- If a solid is heated and changes directly to a gas without melting, i.e. it does not pass through the liquid phase, the change of state is called sublimation.
- We can monitor the change in temperature as a liquid cools down and forms a solid using the apparatus in Figure 3.
- In a heating curve, we monitor the temperature as a solid is heated. The graph obtained is shown in Figure 4.
- When a solid reaches its melting point, the energy we provide in heating the solid is being absorbed to break the forces between the particles in the solid. Boiling a liquid also involves energy being absorbed to separate the particles.

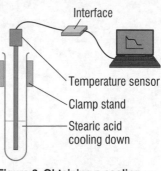

Interface

Temperature sensor

Clamp stand

Stearic acid cooling down

Figure 3 Obtaining a cooling curve

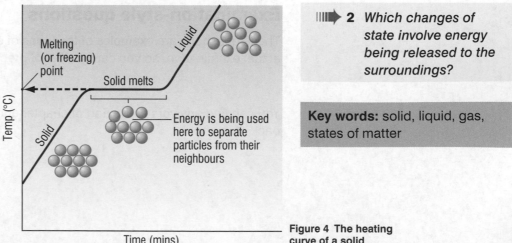

Figure 4 The heating curve of a solid

▸ **2** *Which changes of state involve energy being released to the surroundings?*

Key words: solid, liquid, gas, states of matter

C1.2 Evidence for particles

Key points

- All substances are made up of particles.
- In liquids and gases, the random movement of particles mixes substances in a process called diffusion.
- Diffusion takes place faster in a gas than in a liquid.
- Small, light particles diffuse faster than large, heavy ones.

Figure 1 Bromine vapour diffuses and mixes thoroughly with the air

- All the substances that make up our world are made of tiny particles. These particles are too small to see with the naked eye or even with powerful optical microscopes. However, we do have evidence that they really do exist.
- When baking bread, invisible particles from the hot bread are given off and mix with the gas particles in the air. When particles mix like this it is called **diffusion**.
- Diffusion happens automatically in liquids and gases. You don't need to mix or stir the substances.
- The particles in liquids and gases move constantly in a random manner. Gradually, this has the overall effect of moving particles from an area of **high** concentration to an area of **low** concentration.
- Eventually the diffusing particles will be evenly spread throughout a liquid or throughout a gas in a closed container.

▶ **1** *How can an open bottle of perfume or aftershave give us evidence that matter is made of particles?*

- In experiments such as the one shown below, we find that small, light particles diffuse faster than large, heavy ones.

Demonstration

Diffusion through a gas

Look at the long tube below. This is an experiment to investigate the diffusion of ammonia and hydrogen chloride particles (molecules).

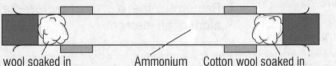

Cotton wool soaked in ammonia solution (concentrated)   Ammonium chloride   Cotton wool soaked in hydrochloric acid (concentrated)

Figure 2 Diffusion of $NH_3(g)$ and $HCl(g)$ through air

After a short time, we see a white smoke of ammonium chloride forming where the ammonia and hydrogen chloride particles meet. They meet nearer the hydrogen chloride end of the tube. They react with each other as shown below:

$$\text{ammonia} + \text{hydrogen chloride} \rightarrow \text{ammonium chloride}$$
$$NH_3(g) + HCl(g) \rightarrow NH_4Cl(s)$$
$$\text{(seen as white 'smoke')}$$

So although we cannot see the particles of ammonia and hydrogen chloride moving through the air in the long tube, we know they have because of the reaction forming the ammonium chloride.

▶ **2** *Look at the experiment above.*
Which has the heavier particles, ammonia or hydrogen chloride? How did you decide?

▶ **3** *Why is diffusion through a liquid slower than diffusion through a gas?*

⊂⊃ links
Revise applying the particle theory in Chapter 8 'Rates of reaction'.

Key word: diffusion

C1.3 Atoms

Key points

- All substances are made of atoms.
- The periodic table lists all the chemical elements, with eight main groups each containing elements with similar chemical properties.
- Elements are made of only one type of atom.
- Compounds contain more than one element.
- An atom has a tiny nucleus at its centre, surrounded by electrons.

Key words: element, atom, group, nucleus, electron, compound

∞ links

Revise more on the patterns in the periodic table in 1.5 'The arrangement of electrons in atoms'.

- There are about 100 different **elements** from which all substances are made. The periodic table is a list of the elements.

▐▶ **1** *What types of substances are shown in the periodic table?*

- Each element is made of only one type of **atom**.
- Atoms are represented by chemical symbols, e.g. Na for an atom of sodium, O for an atom of oxygen.
- The elements in the periodic table are arranged in columns, called groups. The elements in a **group** usually have similar properties.

▐▶ **2** *What atom does the symbol H represent?*

- An atom has a tiny **nucleus** surrounded by **electrons**.
- When elements react, their atoms join with atoms of other elements.
- **Compounds** are formed when two or more elements combine together.

▐▶ **3** *What type of substance is sodium chloride, NaCl?*

Study tip

Remember that a symbol represents one atom of an element.

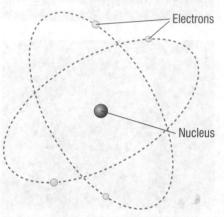

Figure 1 An atom consists of a small nucleus surrounded by electrons

---

Group numbers

1	2											3	4	5	6	7	0
			H 1 Hydrogen														**He** 2 Helium
Li 3 Lithium	**Be** 4 Beryllium											**B** 5 Boron	**C** 6 Carbon	**N** 7 Nitrogen	**O** 8 Oxygen	**F** 9 Fluorine	**Ne** 10 Neon
Na 11 Sodium	**Mg** 12 Magnesium											**Al** 13 Aluminium	**Si** 14 Silicon	**P** 15 Phosphorus	**S** 16 Sulfur	**Cl** 17 Chlorine	**Ar** 18 Argon
K 19 Potassium	**Ca** 20 Calcium	**Sc** 21 Scandium	**Ti** 22 Titanium	**V** 23 Vanadium	**Cr** 24 Chromium	**Mn** 25 Manganese	**Fe** 26 Iron	**Co** 27 Cobalt	**Ni** 28 Nickel	**Cu** 29 Copper	**Zn** 30 Zinc	**Ga** 31 Gallium	**Ge** 32 Germanium	**As** 33 Arsenic	**Se** 34 Selenium	**Br** 35 Bromine	**Kr** 36 Krypton
Rb 37 Rubidium	**Sr** 38 Strontium	**Y** 39 Yttrium	**Zr** 40 Zirconium	**Nb** 41 Niobium	**Mo** 42 Molybdenum	**Tc** 43 Technetium	**Ru** 44 Ruthenium	**Rh** 45 Rhodium	**Pd** 46 Palladium	**Ag** 47 Silver	**Cd** 48 Cadmium	**In** 49 Indium	**Sn** 50 Tin	**Sb** 51 Antimony	**Te** 52 Tellurium	**I** 53 Iodine	**Xe** 54 Xenon
Cs 55 Caesium	**Ba** 56 Barium	Lanthanum see below	**Hf** 72 Hafnium	**Ta** 73 Tantalum	**W** 74 Tungsten	**Re** 75 Rhenium	**Os** 76 Osmium	**Ir** 77 Iridium	**Pt** 78 Platinum	**Au** 79 Gold	**Hg** 80 Mercury	**Tl** 81 Thallium	**Pb** 82 Lead	**Bi** 83 Bismuth	**Po** 84 Polonium	**At** 85 Astatine	**Rn** 86 Radon
Fr 87 Francium	**Ra** 88 Radium	Actinium see below															

↑ The transition metals

↑ The halogens ↑ The noble gases

The alkali metals

The alkaline earth metals

Lanthanides

La 57 Lanthanium	**Ce** 58 Cerium	**Pr** 59 Praseodymium	**Nd** 60 Neodymium	**Pm** 61 Promethium	**Sm** 62 Samarium	**Eu** 63 Europium	**Gd** 64 Gadolinium	**Tb** 65 Terbium	**Dy** 66 Dysprosium	**Ho** 67 Holmium	**Er** 68 Erbium	**Tm** 69 Thulium	**Yb** 70 Ytterbium	**Lu** 71 Lutetium

Actinides

Ac 89 Actinium	**Th** 90 Thorium	**Pa** 91 Protactinium	**U** 92 Uranium	**Np** 93 Neptunium	**Pu** 94 Plutonium	**Am** 95 Americium	**Cm** 96 Curium	**Bk** 97 Berkelium	**Cf** 98 Californium	**Es** 99 Einsteinium	**Fm** 100 Fermium	**Md** 101 Mendelevium	**No** 102 Nobelium	**Lr** 103 Lawrencium

Figure 2 The periodic table shows the symbols of the elements

C1.4 Atomic structure

Key points

- Atoms are made of protons, neutrons and electrons.

- Protons have a relative charge of +1, and electrons have a relative charge of –1. Neutrons have no electric charge. They are neutral.

- Atoms contain an equal number of protons and electrons so carry no overall charge.

- Atomic number = number of protons (= number of electrons).

- Mass number = number of protons + neutrons.

- Atoms of the same element have the same number of protons (and hence electrons) in their atoms.

links

To revise more on the patterns in the periodic table see 1.5 'The arrangement of electrons in atoms'.

Study tip

In an atom, the number of protons is always equal to the number of electrons. You can find out the number of protons and electrons in an atom by looking up its atomic number in the periodic table.

- The nucleus at the centre of an atom contains two types of particle. These are called **protons** and **neutrons**. Protons have a positive charge and neutrons have no charge.

- Electrons are tiny negatively charged particles that move around the nucleus. An atom has no overall charge. That is because the number of protons is equal to the number of electrons and their charges are equal and opposite (proton +1 and electron –1).

▶ **1** *Why are atoms neutral?*

- All atoms of an element contain the same number of protons. This number is called the **atomic number** (or proton number) of the element. Elements are arranged in order of their atomic numbers in the periodic table. The atomic number is also the number of electrons in an atom of the element.

- The **mass number** is the total number of particles in the nucleus of an atom, so it is the number of protons plus the number of neutrons.

▶ **2** *How many protons, neutrons and electrons are there in an atom of aluminium (atomic number 13, mass number 27)?*

Maths skills

Work out the number of each type of particle in an atom of fluorine from its atomic number of 9 and its mass number of 19.

Number of protons = atomic number = 9

Number of electrons = number of protons = 9

Number of neutrons = mass number – atomic number = 19 – 9 = 10

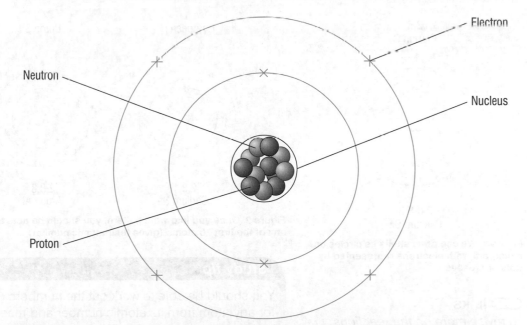

Figure 1 Understanding the structure of an atom gives us important clues to the way substances react together

Key words: proton, neutron, atomic number, mass number

C1.5

The arrangement of electrons in atoms

- The atoms of the unreactive noble gases (in Group 0) all have very stable arrangements of electrons.
- Electrons in atoms are in energy levels that can be represented by shells.
- Electrons in the lowest energy level are in the shell closest to the nucleus.
- Electrons occupy the lowest energy levels first.
- All the elements in the same group of the periodic table have the same number of electrons in their highest energy level (outer shell).

- Each electron in an atom is in an **energy level**. Energy levels can be represented as **shells**, with electrons in the lowest energy level closest to the nucleus.
- The lowest energy level or first shell can hold two electrons, and the second energy level can hold eight. Electrons occupy the lowest possible energy levels. The **electronic structure** of neon with 10 electrons is 2,8. Sodium with 11 electrons has the electronic structure 2,8,1.

> **1** *Draw a diagram to show the electronic structure of an atom of aluminium (atomic number 13).*

- Elements in the same group of the periodic table have the same number of electrons in their highest energy level. For example, Group 1 elements have one electron in their highest energy level.

> **2** *Explain why nitrogen and phosphorus are both in Group 5 of the periodic table.*

- Group 1 elements include lithium, sodium and potassium. These elements react quickly with water and with oxygen.
- The atoms of the unreactive noble gases (in Group 0) all have very stable arrangements of electrons.

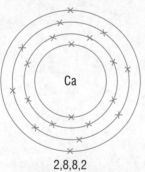

Figure 1 We can draw shells as circles on a diagram, with electrons represented by dots or crosses

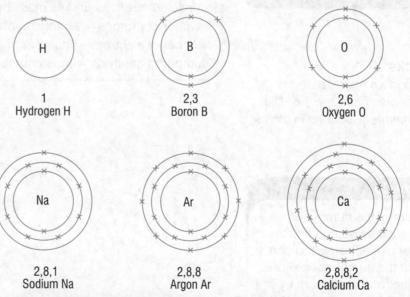

Figure 2 Once you know the pattern, you should be able to draw the energy levels of the electrons in any of the first 20 atoms (given their atomic number)

⚭ links

To revise more on the reactions of elements and their electronic structures see Chapter 5 'The periodic table'.

Study tip

You should be able to work out the numbers of protons, neutrons and electrons for any atom from its atomic number and mass number.

Key words: energy level, shell, electronic structure

Student Book
pages 12–13

C1.6 Atoms and isotopes

Key points

- The relative mass of protons and neutrons is 1.
- We can represent the atomic number and mass number of an atom using the notation: $^{24}_{12}Mg$, where magnesium's atomic number is 12 and its mass number is 24.
- Isotopes are atoms of the same element with different numbers of neutrons. They have identical chemical properties, but their physical properties, such as density, can differ.

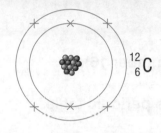

- Proton — Number of protons gives atomic number
- Neutron — Number of protons plus number of neutrons gives mass number

Figure 2 An atom of carbon

- Protons and neutrons have the same mass and so the relative masses of a proton and a neutron are both one.
- The mass of an electron is very small compared with a proton or neutron, and so the mass of an atom is made up almost entirely of its protons and neutrons. The total number of protons and neutrons in an atom is called its **mass number**.

▐▶ **1** *Why do we count only protons and neutrons to calculate the mass number of an atom?*

- Atoms of the same element all have the same **atomic number**. The number of protons and electrons in an atom must always be the same, but there can be different numbers of neutrons.
- Atoms of the same element with different numbers of neutrons are called **isotopes**.
- The number of neutrons in an atom is equal to its mass number minus its atomic number. We can show the mass number and atomic number of an atom like this:

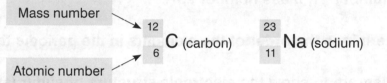

Mass number

$^{12}_{6}C$ (carbon) $^{23}_{11}Na$ (sodium)

Atomic number

Figure 1 Showing the mass number and atomic number

- The number at the top is the mass number (which is larger than the atomic number, except for hydrogen, $^{1}_{1}H$). So this sodium atom has 11 protons, 11 electrons and (23 − 11) = 12 neutrons.

▐▶ **2** *How many protons, electrons and neutrons are there in an atom of $^{19}_{9}F$?*

Study tip

Remember that isotopes are atoms of the same element. They have the same chemical properties but they have different physical properties because of their different masses. Some isotopes are unstable and radioactive.

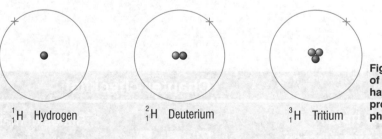

$^{1}_{1}H$ Hydrogen $^{2}_{1}H$ Deuterium $^{3}_{1}H$ Tritium

Figure 3 The isotopes of hydrogen – they have identical chemical properties but different physical properties

▐▶ **3** *What are isotopes?*

Key words: mass number, atomic number, isotope

1. Which of the following changes of state involve energy being absorbed from the surroundings and which involve energy being released to the surroundings?

   boiling, melting, condensing, freezing

2. Describe the movement in the particles of a solid.

3. What do we call the process whereby the particles in a one gas mix and spread out evenly with the particles of another gas in a closed container?

4. Sort these substances into elements and compounds:

   Ca, CH_4, H_2, HCl, MgO, Ne, O_2, SO_2.

5. What are the names and numbers of the subatomic particles in an atom of sodium (atomic number 11, mass number 23)?

6. What determines the order of the elements in the periodic table?

7. Draw a diagram to show the electronic structure of sulfur (atomic number 16).

8. Explain why boron and aluminium are both in the same group in the periodic table.

9. Given the atomic number and mass number of an atom, explain how to work out the number of neutrons in the nucleus of the atom.

10. There are two main types of chlorine atom, $^{35}_{17}Cl$ and $^{37}_{17}Cl$.

    a What name is used for these two types of atom?

    b Explain how an atom of $^{35}_{17}Cl$ differs from an atom of $^{37}_{17}Cl$?

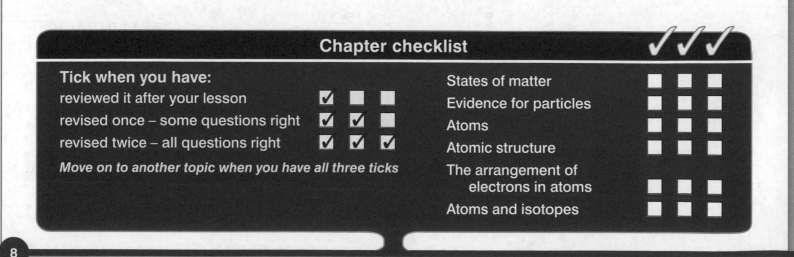

Chapter checklist

Tick when you have:							
reviewed it after your lesson	✔	☐	☐	States of matter	☐	☐	☐
revised once – some questions right	✔	✔	☐	Evidence for particles	☐	☐	☐
revised twice – all questions right	✔	✔	✔	Atoms	☐	☐	☐
				Atomic structure	☐	☐	☐
Move on to another topic when you have all three ticks				The arrangement of electrons in atoms	☐	☐	☐
				Atoms and isotopes	☐	☐	☐

C2.1 Relative masses and moles

Key points

- We compare the masses of atoms by measuring them relative to atoms of carbon-12.

- We work out the relative formula mass of a compound by adding up the relative atomic masses of the elements in it, in the ratio shown by its formula.

- One mole of any substance is its relative formula mass, in grams.

- Number of moles =
  $$\frac{mass\ (g)}{A_r}\ or\ \frac{mass\ (g)}{M_r}$$

Maths skills

Worked example

Calculate the M_r of calcium chloride, $CaCl_2$

Answer

A_r of Ca = 40, A_r of Cl = 35.5, so $M_r = 40 + (35.5 \times 2) = $ **111**

Study tip

Make sure you can calculate the relative formula mass (M_r) of a compound from its formula. Practise calculating the mass of one mole of different substances from their formula and the relative atomic masses that you are given, as well as the number of moles in a given mass of substance.

- Atoms are much too small to weigh and so we use their **relative atomic mass** (A_r) in calculations. Relative atomic masses are often shown in periodic tables. In the laboratory we usually weigh substances in grams. The relative atomic mass of an element in grams is called one **mole** of atoms of the element.

▶ **1** *What is the mass of one mole of sodium atoms?*

- We use an atom of $^{12}_{6}C$ as a standard atom and compare the masses of all other atoms with this. The relative atomic mass of an element (A_r) is an average value that depends on the isotopes the element contains. However, when rounded to a whole number it is often the same as the mass number of the main isotope of the element.

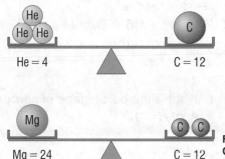

He = 4   C = 12

Mg = 24   C = 12

Figure 1 The relative mass of $^{12}_{6}C$ atom is 12. Compared with this, the A_r of helium is 4 and the A_r of magnesium is 24.

▶ **2** *Why is the relative atomic mass of chlorine not a whole number?*

- The relative formula mass (M_r) of a substance is found by adding up the relative atomic masses of the atoms in its formula.

▶ **3** *Calculate the relative formula mass (M_r) of sodium sulfate, Na_2SO_4. (Relative atomic masses: Na = 23, S = 32, O = 16).*

- The **relative formula mass** (M_r) of a substance in grams is called one mole of that substance. Using moles of substances is useful when we need to work out how much of a substance reacts or how much product we will get.

Maths skills

Worked example

What is the mass of one mole of sodium hydroxide, NaOH?

Answer

A_r of Na = 23, A_r of O = 16, A_r of H = 1, so 1 mole NaOH = (23 + 16 + 1)g = 40g

▶ **4** *What is the mass of one mole of magnesium carbonate, $MgCO_3$? (Relative atomic masses: Mg = 24, C = 12, O = 16).*

Key words: relative atomic mass (A_r), mole, relative formula mass (M_r)

Student Book
pages 18–19

C2.2 Percentages and formulae

Key points

- The relative atomic masses of the elements in a compound and its formula can be used to work out its percentage composition.
- We can calculate empirical formulae given the masses or percentage composition of elements present.

- We can calculate the percentage of any of the elements in a compound from the formula of the compound. Divide the relative atomic mass of the element by the relative formula mass of the compound and multiply the answer by 100 to convert it to a percentage. This can be useful when deciding if a compound is suitable for a particular purpose or to identify a compound.

Maths skills

Worked example

What is the percentage of carbon in carbon dioxide, CO_2?

Answer

A_r of C = 12, A_r of O = 16
M_r of CO_2 = 12 + (16 × 2) = 44
So percentage of carbon = (12/44) × 100 = **27.3%**

▶ **1** *What is the percentage of carbon in methane, CH_4? (A_r of C = 12, A_r of H = 1).*

Study tip

When calculating an empirical formula it is helpful to set out your answer in a table. In the exam you should always show your working in calculations.

Working out the formula of a compound from its percentage composition

- The **empirical formula** is the simplest ratio of the atoms or ions in a compound. It is the formula used for ionic compounds, but for covalent compounds it is not always the same as the **molecular formula**. For example, the molecular formula of ethane is C_2H_6, but its empirical formula is CH_3.
- We can calculate the empirical formula of a compound from its percentage composition:

Divide the mass of each element in 100 g of the compound by its A_r to give the ratio of atoms. Then convert this to the simplest whole number ratio.

Maths skills

Worked example

What is the empirical formula of the hydrocarbon that contains 80% carbon?

Answer

	Carbon	Hydrogen
Mass in 100 g of compound	80	20
Ratio of atoms or moles of atoms (mass/A_r)	80/12 = 6.67	20/1 = 20
Simplest ratio of atoms (divide by smallest)	6.67/6.67 = 1	20/6.67 = 3
Empirical formula		**CH₃**

▶ **2** *What is the empirical formula of the compound that contains 70% iron and 30% oxygen? (A_r of Fe = 56, A_r of O = 16)*

Figure 1 A small difference in the amount of metal in an ore might not seem very much. However, when millions of tonnes of ore are extracted and processed each year, it all adds up!

Key words: empirical formula, molecular formula

C2.3 Chemical equations

Key points

- As no new atoms are ever created or destroyed in a chemical reaction:
  the total mass of reactants = the total mass of products
- There is the same number of each type of atom on each side of a balanced symbol equation.
- We can include state symbols to give extra information in balanced symbol equations. These are (s) for solids, (l) for liquids, (g) for gases and (aq) for aqueous solutions.

- In chemical reactions the atoms in the **reactants** rearrange themselves to form new substances, the **products**.
- Atoms are neither created nor destroyed in a chemical reaction. So the number and type of atoms remain the same before and after the reaction.
- This means that the mass of the products equals the mass of reactants.
- It also means that we can write chemical equations to represent reactions.
- Word equations only give the names of the reactants and products. Symbol equations show the numbers and types of atoms in the reactants and products.
- When symbol equations are written they should always be balanced.
- This means that the numbers of each type of atom should be the same on both sides of a symbol equation.
- We can also include state symbols in balanced symbol equations. These are (s) for solids, (l) for liquids, (g) for gases and (aq) for aqueous solutions.

▐▶ 1 *Explain as fully as you can what this balanced symbol equation tells you:*

$$Mg + 2HCl \rightarrow MgCl_2 + H_2$$

Making an equation balance

Symbol equations are balanced by changing the large numbers in front of the formulae of the reactants and products. You should balance equations by changing only the large numbers. Never change the small (subscript) numbers because this changes the formula of the substance. (See Figure 1.)

▐▶ 2 *Balance these equations:*
   a $H_2 + Cl_2 \rightarrow HCl$
   b $Na + O_2 \rightarrow Na_2O$
   c $Na_2CO_3 + HCl \rightarrow NaCl + H_2O + CO_2$

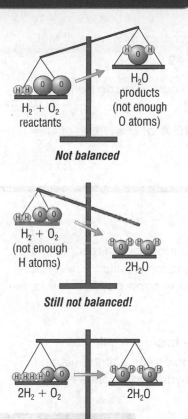

Not balanced

Still not balanced!

Balanced at last!

Figure 1 Making an equation balance

Study tip

Remember that in a balanced symbol equation a large number multiplies all of the atoms in the formula that follows.

Maths skills

In the formulae in symbol equations, small (subscript) numbers multiply only the atom they follow. For example: In H_2SO_4 we have H_2 = 2 atoms of hydrogen, S = one atom of sulfur, O_4 = 4 atoms of oxygen.

If more than one atom within a formula has to be multiplied, brackets are used. $Mg(NO_3)_2$ (one magnesium ion and two nitrate ions) is made from one atom of magnesium; 1×2 atoms of nitrogen; $3 \times 2 = 6$ atoms of oxygen.

Large numbers multiply all atoms in the formula that follows. So $2CO_2$ (two molecules of carbon dioxide) shows a total of two carbon atoms and four oxygen atoms.

∞ links

Revise more about solids, liquids and gases in 1.1 'States of matter'.

Key words: reactant, product

Student Book
pages 22–23

C2.4 Equations and calculations

Calculating masses from chemical equations

Key points

- Balanced symbol equations tell us the number of moles of substances involved in a chemical reaction.

- We can use balanced symbol equations to calculate the masses of reactants and products in a chemical reaction.

- Chemical equations show the reactants and products of a reaction. When they are balanced they show the amounts of atoms, molecules or ions in the reaction. For example: $2Mg + O_2 \rightarrow 2MgO$ shows that two atoms of magnesium react with one molecule of oxygen to form two magnesium ions and two oxide ions. If we work in moles, the equation tells us that two moles of magnesium atoms react with one mole of oxygen molecules to produce two moles of magnesium oxide. This means that 48 g of magnesium react with 32 g of oxygen to give 80 g of magnesium oxide. (A_r of Mg = 24, A_r of O = 16)

- Alternatively, if we work in relative masses from the equation: $(2 \times A_r$ of Mg$) + (2 \times A_r$ of O$)$ gives $(2 \times M_r$ of MgO$)$. Converting this to grams it becomes (2×24) g Mg + (2×16) g O gives (2×40) g MgO, or 48 g Mg + 32 g O gives 80 g MgO (which is the same as when we used moles). If we have 5 g of magnesium, we can work out the mass of magnesium oxide it will produce using ratios: 1 g Mg will produce 80/48 g MgO so 5 g Mg will produce $5 \times 80/48$ g MgO = 8.33 g of MgO

- If we use moles the calculation can be done like this:
1 mole of Mg produces 1 mole of MgO
5 g Mg = 5/24 mole of magnesium and so it will produce 5/24 mole of MgO
The mass of 5/24 mole MgO = $5/24 \times 40$ g = **8.33 g** of MgO

Study tip

You can work in moles or you can use relative masses when doing calculations, but if you are asked to calculate a mass of a reactant or product do not forget to give the correct units in your answer.

> **1** *Calculate the mass of calcium oxide that can be made from 10 g of calcium carbonate in the reaction:*
>
> $CaCO_3 \rightarrow CaO + CO_2$ *(A_r of Ca = 40, A_r of O = 16, A_r of C = 12)*

∞ links

Revise more about calculations that are based on balanced equations in 6.6 'Titration calculations'.

Student Book
pages 24–25

C2.5 Reversible reactions

- In a reversible reaction the products of the reaction can react to make the original reactants.

- We can show a reversible reaction using the sign ⇌.

- If the products of a chemical reaction can react to produce the reactants, the reaction can go in both directions. This type of reaction is called a **reversible reaction** and is represented with the symbol ⇌. One arrow points in the forwards direction (to the right) and one backwards.

- An example of a reversible reaction is:

ammonium chloride ⇌ ammonia + hydrogen chloride

- When heated, ammonium chloride decomposes to produce ammonia and hydrogen chloride. When cooled, ammonia and hydrogen chloride react to produce ammonium chloride.

> **1** *What is a reversible reaction?*

∞ links

Revise more about reversible reactions in 12.3 'Energy and reversible reactions'.

Key word: reversible reaction

Study tip

You should know that the thermal decomposition of ammonium chloride is just one example of a reversible reaction and that there are many others. You do not have to remember any other examples but may be given information about other reversible reactions in the exam.

Figure 1 Heating ammonium chloride: an example of a reversible reaction

Student Book
pages 26–27

C2.6

The yield of a chemical reaction

- The **yield** of a chemical process is how much you actually make. The **percentage yield** compares the amount made with the maximum amount that could be made, calculated as a percentage.

Key points

- The yield of a chemical reaction describes how much product is made.
- The percentage yield of a chemical reaction tells us how much product is made compared with the maximum amount that could be made (100%).
- Factors affecting the yield of a chemical reaction include product being left behind in the apparatus, reversible reactions not going to completion, some reactants may produce unexpected reactions, and losses in separating the products from the reaction mixture.

⚬⚬ *links*
Revise more about using balanced symbol equations to predict reacting masses in 2.4 'Equations and calculations'.

Calculating percentage yield

The percentage yield is calculated using this equation:

$$\text{Percentage yield} = \frac{\text{(amount of product collected}}{\text{maximum amount of product possible)}} \times 100\%$$

The maximum amount of product possible is calculated from the balanced equation for the reaction.

For example: A student collected 2.3 g of magnesium oxide from 2.0 g of magnesium.

Theoretically: $2Mg + O_2 \rightarrow 2MgO$, so 48 g of Mg should give 80 g of MgO, and so 2.0 g of Mg should give $2 \times 80/48 = 3.33$ g of MgO.

$$\text{Percentage yield} = \left(\frac{2.3}{3.33}\right) \times 100 = \mathbf{69\%}$$

Study tip

You should be able to calculate the percentage yield of a reaction from information about the mass of product obtained and the equation for the reaction.

▐▶ **1** *A student made 4.4 g of calcium oxide from 4.0 g of calcium heated in air. Calculate the percentage yield.*

- When you actually do chemical reactions it is not usually possible to collect the amounts calculated from the balanced symbol equations. Reactions may not go to completion, other reactions may happen and some product may be lost when it is separated or collected from the apparatus.

▐▶ **2** *Why is it not usually possible to get 100% yield from a chemical reaction?*

- Using reactions with high yields in industry helps to conserve resources and to reduce waste. Chemical processes should also waste as little energy as possible. Working in these ways helps to reduce pollution and makes production more sustainable.

▐▶ **3** *Why should chemical manufacturers use reactions with high yields?*

Key words: yield, percentage yield

1 Calcium carbonate decomposes when heated to produce calcium oxide and carbon dioxide. 20.0 g of calcium carbonate produced 11.2 g of calcium oxide. What mass of carbon dioxide would be produced?

2 Hydrogen and iodine react to make hydrogen iodide. The equation for the reaction is:

$$H_2 + I_2 \rightleftharpoons 2HI$$

What type of reaction is this?

3 Write the word equation and the balanced symbol equation, including state symbols, for the reactions taking place when solid ammonium chloride (NH_4Cl) is heated in a test tube.

4 The equation for a reaction of lead nitrate is:

$$Pb(NO_3)_2 + 2KI \rightarrow 2KNO_3 + PbI_2$$

a Write a word equation for this reaction.

b Give the name and number of each type of atom in the products.

5 What is the relative formula mass of magnesium fluoride, MgF_2?

6 What is the mass of one mole of aluminium oxide, Al_2O_3?

7 What is the percentage by mass of copper in copper(II) carbonate, $CuCO_3$?

8 A student made some magnesium oxide by burning magnesium in air. The student obtained a yield of 55%. Suggest two reasons why the yield was less than 100%.

9 What is the empirical formula of vanadium oxide that contains 56% of vanadium?

10 Calculate the mass of zinc chloride that you can make from 6.5 g of zinc.

$$Zn + 2HCl \rightarrow ZnCl_2 + H_2$$

11 Calculate the percentage yield if 9.0 g $MgSO_4$ was made from 4.0 g MgO reacting with excess dilute sulfuric acid (H_2SO_4).

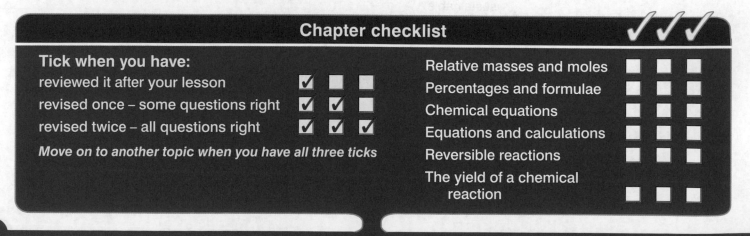

Chapter checklist

Tick when you have:
reviewed it after your lesson ☑ ☐ ☐
revised once – some questions right ☑ ☑ ☐
revised twice – all questions right ☑ ☑ ☑

Move on to another topic when you have all three ticks

Relative masses and moles ☐ ☐ ☐
Percentages and formulae ☐ ☐ ☐
Chemical equations ☐ ☐ ☐
Equations and calculations ☐ ☐ ☐
Reversible reactions ☐ ☐ ☐
The yield of a chemical reaction ☐ ☐ ☐

1 Lithium metal (Li) reacts with chlorine gas (Cl_2) when heated to form solid lithium chloride (LiCl).

  a Write a balanced symbol equation, including state symbols, for the reaction of lithium metal with chlorine gas. *(2 marks)*

  b i The atomic number of lithium is 3. What does this tell us about the subatomic particles in an atom of lithium? *(2 marks)*

    ii The atomic number of chlorine is 17. Draw a diagram to show the arrangement of the electrons in an atom of lithium and in an atom of chlorine. *(3 marks)*

  c The experiment to make lithium chloride from lithium and chlorine gas should be carried out in a fume cupboard. Explain why. *(1 mark)*

  d Chlorine gas contains two isotopes of chlorine.

    i What are 'isotopes'? *(1 mark)*

    ii One isotope of chlorine has a mass number of 35 and the other has a mass number of 37. What is the difference between the atomic structures of the two isotopes? *(1 mark)*

2 When sodium nitrate(v), $NaNO_3$, is heated in a test tube, it breaks down to form sodium nitrate(III) ($NaNO_2$) and oxygen (O_2). Both sodium nitrate(v) and sodium nitrate(III) are white solids.

Sodium nitrate(v)

Heat

  a Copy and complete the diagram to show oxygen being collected over water in a test tube. *(3 marks)*

    i When no more oxygen is given off, heating is continued until the end of the delivery tube is raised above the surface of the water. Why? *(2 marks)*

    ii How can you test that the gas given off is oxygen? *(2 marks)*

  b Write a balanced symbol equation, including state symbols, for the reaction taking place when sodium nitrate(v) is heated. *(2 marks)*

  c i The experiment was carried out with 8.5 g of sodium nitrate(v). Using your answer to part b, calculate the mass of sodium nitrate(III) that should be left in the test tube after the reaction is complete. (Relative atomic masses: Na = 23, N = 14, O = 16) *(3 marks)*

    ii In the experiment, the sodium nitrate(v) was heated for two minutes. The mass of white solid left in the test tube was greater than that expected by calculation. Give a reason why this might happen. *(1 mark)*

3 A compound containing potassium, bromine and oxygen was analysed in a laboratory in order to find its empirical formula.

33.4 g of the compound was found to contain 7.8 g of potassium and 16.0 g of bromine. (Relative atomic masses: K = 39, Br = 80, O = 16)

  a Work out the mass of oxygen in the compound analysed. *(1 mark)*

  b i What does an empirical formula tell us about a compound? *(1 mark)*

    ii Calculate the empirical formula of the compound analysed. *(4 marks)*

  c What other piece of information is needed to confirm if an empirical formula is the same as the molecular formula of a compound? *(1 mark)*

  d The compound analysed is a white crystalline solid at room temperature. Describe the arrangement and movement of its particles in the solid state. *(2 marks)*

  e Another compound of potassium, bromine and oxygen was analysed and was found to contain 29% potassium and 59% bromine.

    i What percentage of the compound was oxygen? *(1 mark)*

    ii What is the empirical formula of this compound? *(3 marks)*

Study tip

Question 2 is the type of question found in Paper 2 of the examination. It requires you to apply our knowledge of practical chemistry.

Study tip

Ensure you show the steps in your working out for parts **bii** and **eii**.

C3.1 Atoms into ions

Key points

- Elements react to form compounds by gaining or losing electrons, or by sharing electrons.

- The elements in Group 1 react with the elements in Group 7. As they react, atoms of Group 1 elements can each lose one electron to gain the stable electronic structure of a noble gas. This electron can be given to an atom from Group 7, which then also achieves the stable electronic structure of a noble gas.

- When two or more elements react together compounds are formed. The atoms of elements join together by sharing electrons or by transferring electrons to achieve stable electronic structures. Atoms of the noble gases have stable electronic structures.

- When atoms of non-metallic elements join together by sharing electrons it is called **covalent bonding**.

▷ 1 How can you tell that the compound H_2O has covalent bonds?

- When metallic elements react with non-metallic elements they produce ionic compounds. The metal atoms lose electrons to form positive **ions**. The atoms of non-metals gain electrons to form negative ions. The ions have the stable electronic structure of a noble gas. The oppositely charged ions attract each other in the ionic compound and this is called **ionic bonding**.

▷ 2 Which of these compounds have ionic bonding?
  $KBr, HCl, H_2S, Na_2O, Cl_2O, MgO$

- Elements in Group 1 of the periodic table have atoms with one electron in their highest occupied energy level (outer shell). Sodium atoms, Na, (electronic structure 2,8,1), form sodium ions, Na^+ (electronic structure 2,8).

- Elements in Group 7 of the periodic table have atoms with seven electrons in their highest occupied energy level (outer shell). Chlorine atoms, Cl (2,8,7) form chloride ions, Cl^- (2,8,8).

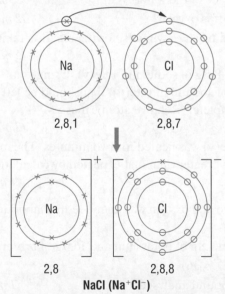

Figure 1 The formation of sodium chloride (NaCl) is an example of ion formation by transferring an electron

- The compound sodium chloride has equal numbers of sodium ions and chloride ions and so we write its formula as NaCl.

▷ 3 Explain what happens to the atoms of the elements when lithium reacts with fluorine.

Key words: covalent bonding, ion, ionic bonding

C3.2 Ionic bonding

Key points

- Ionic compounds are held together by strong forces of attraction between the oppositely charged ions. This is called ionic bonding.
- Besides the elements in Groups 1 and 7, other elements that can form ionic compounds include those from Groups 2 and 6.

- Ionic bonding holds oppositely charged ions together in **giant structures**. The giant structure of ionic compounds is very regular because the ions all pack together neatly, like marbles in a box.
- Strong electrostatic forces of attraction act in all directions. Each ion in the giant structure or lattice is surrounded by ions with the opposite charge and so is held firmly in place.
- Sodium chloride contains equal numbers of sodium ions and chloride ions as shown by its formula NaCl. The sodium ions and chloride ions form a cubic **lattice**.
- The ratio of ions in the structure of an ionic compound depends on the charges on the ions. For example, calcium ions are Ca^{2+} and chloride ions are Cl^-, so calcium chloride contains twice as many chloride ions as calcium ions and its formula is $CaCl_2$.

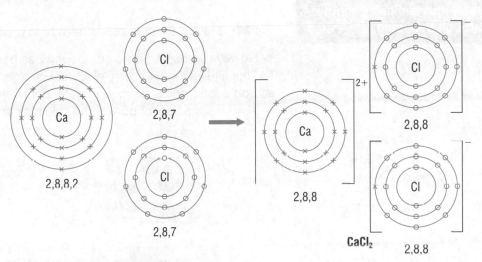

Figure 2 The formation of calcium chloride (CaCl₂)

- Oxygen atoms (2,6) from Group 6 gain two electrons to form O^{2-} ions (2,8) when it reacts with calcium atoms (2,8,8,2) from Group 2. So the formula of the ionic compound calcium oxide is CaO.

▷ **1** *Why is the formula of sodium chloride NaCl but magnesium chloride is MgCl₂?*

Study tip

The ionic bonds should not be confused with electron transfer between atoms (which is how ions form) – the ionic bonds arise because of the attraction between oppositely charged ions.

⚭ links

To revise more about Group 1 elements see 5.2 'Group 1 – The Alkali metals' and the Group 7 elements in 5.4 'Group 7 – the halogens'.

Key words: giant structure, lattice

C3.3 Giant ionic structures

Key points

- It takes a lot of energy to break the many strong ionic bonds that hold a giant ionic lattice together. So ionic compounds have high melting points. They are all solids at room temperature.

- Ionic compounds will conduct electricity when we melt them or dissolve them in water. That's because their ions can then move around freely and can carry charge through the liquid.

- Ionic compounds have giant structures in which many strong electrostatic forces hold the ions together. This means they are solids at room temperature. A lot of energy is needed to overcome the ionic bonds to melt the solids. Therefore ionic compounds have high melting points and high boiling points.

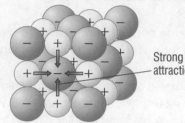

Strong electrostatic forces of attraction called ionic bonds

Figure 1 There are very strong electrostatic forces of attraction in ionic compounds

1 *Why do ionic solids have high melting points?*

- However, when an ionic compound has been melted the ions are free to move. This allows them to carry electrical charge, so the liquids conduct electricity.
- Some ionic solids dissolve in water because water molecules can split up the lattice. The ions are free to move in the solutions and so they also conduct electricity.

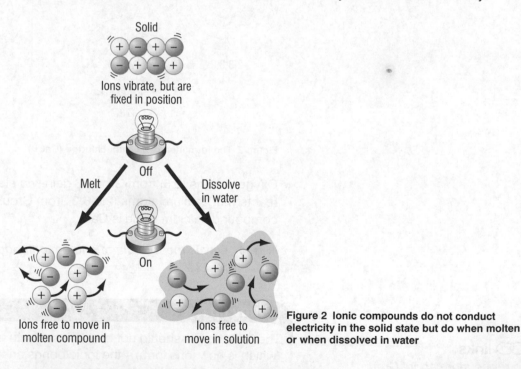

Solid

Ions vibrate, but are fixed in position

Off

Melt   Dissolve in water

On

Ions free to move in molten compound

Ions free to move in solution

Figure 2 Ionic compounds do not conduct electricity in the solid state but do when molten or when dissolved in water

2 *Why can ionic substances conduct electricity when molten or when dissolved in water?*

links

Revise the movement and arrangement of particles in solids and liquid in 1.1 'States of matter'.

Study tip

Remember that every ionic compound is made up of a giant structure of oppositely charged ions.

Covalent bonding

Key points

- A covalent bond is formed when two atoms share a pair of electrons.

- The number of covalent bonds an atom forms depends on the number of electrons it needs to achieve a stable electronic structure.

- Many substances containing covalent bonds consist of simple molecules, but some have giant covalent structures.

- The atoms of non-metals need to gain electrons to achieve stable electronic structures. They can do this by sharing electrons with other atoms. Each shared pair of electrons strongly attracts the two atoms, forming a covalent bond. Substances that have atoms held together by covalent bonding are called molecules.

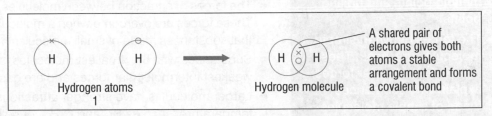

Figure 1 Hydrogen gas is made up of H_2 molecules. Both H atoms in the H_2 molecule gain the stable electronic structure of the noble gas helium by sharing a pair of electrons.

- A covalent bond acts only between the two atoms it bonds to each other, and so many covalently bonded substances consist of small molecules. Sometimes a molecule can contain double (or triple) covalent bonds, as in the oxygen molecule, O_2. shown below:

Figure 2 Oxygen gas is made up of O_2 molecules. Both O atoms in the O_2 molecule gain the stable electronic structure of the noble gas neon by sharing two pairs of electrons in a double covalent bond, often shown as O=O.

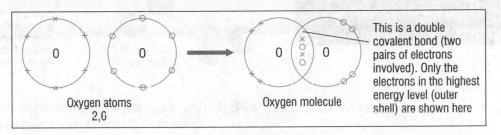

- Atoms of elements in Group 7 need to gain one electron and so form a single covalent bond. Atoms of elements in Group 6 need to gain two electrons and so form two covalent bonds. Atoms of elements in Group 5 can form three bonds and those in Group 4 can form four bonds.

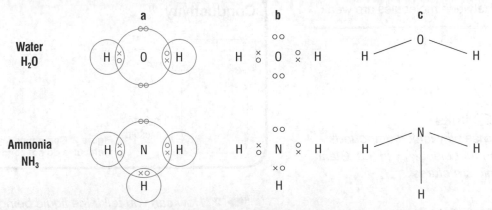

Figure 3 We can represent a covalent compound by showing: a the highest energy levels (or outer shells), b the outer electrons in a dot-and-cross diagram, or c the number of covalent bonds

Study tip

Covalent bonds join atoms together to form molecules. You should only use the word molecule when describing substances that are covalently bonded.

▷ **1** *Draw diagrams using symbols and lines to show the covalent bonds in: chlorine Cl_2, hydrogen chloride HCl, hydrogen sulfide H_2S, oxygen O_2 and carbon dioxide CO_2.*

- Some atoms that can form several bonds, such as carbon, can join together in giant covalent structures. These giant covalent structures are sometimes referred to as macromolecules.

C3.5 Simple molecules

Key points

- Substances made up of simple molecules have low melting points and boiling points.

- The forces between simple molecules are weak. These weak intermolecular forces explain why substances made of simple molecules have low melting points and boiling points.

- Simple molecules have no overall charge, so they cannot carry electrical charge. Therefore substances made of simple molecules do not conduct electricity.

- The atoms within a molecule are held together by strong covalent bonds. These bonds act only between the atoms within the molecule, and so simple molecules have little attraction for each other. Substances made of simple molecules have relatively low melting points and boiling points.

- The forces of attraction between molecules, called **intermolecular forces**, are weak. These forces are overcome when a molecular substance melts or boils. This means that substances made of small molecules have low melting and boiling points.

- Substances with the smallest molecules, such as H_2, Cl_2 and CH_4, have the weakest intermolecular forces and are gases at room temperature.

- Larger molecules have stronger attractions and so may be liquids at room temperature, such as Br_2 and C_6H_{14}, or solids with low melting points, such as I_2.

- Look at the molecules in a sample of chlorine, Cl_2, gas:

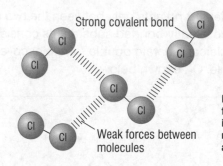

Strong covalent bond

Weak forces between molecules

Figure 1 This shows the covalent bonds and the weak forces between molecules in chlorine gas. It is the weak intermolecular forces that are overcome when substances made of simple molecules melt or boil. The covalent bonds are NOT broken.

> 1 **Why are substances with larger molecules more likely to be liquids or solids than gases at room temperature?**

Study tip

Although the covalent bonds in molecules are strong, the forces between molecules are weak.

- The conductivity of liquids can be tested as shown below:

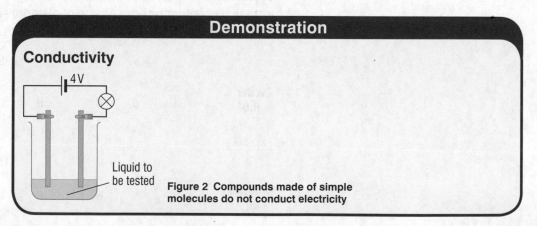

Demonstration

Conductivity

4 V

Liquid to be tested

Figure 2 Compounds made of simple molecules do not conduct electricity

links

Revise why ionic compounds conduct electricity in 3.3 'Giant ionic structures'.

> 2 **How can you tell if the liquid being tested in the apparatus above conducts electricity or not?**

- Simple molecules do not conduct electricity because there is no overall charge on the simple molecules in a compound such as ethanol. Therefore their neutral molecules cannot carry electrical charge.

> 3 **Why does ethanol not conduct electricity?**

Key word: intermolecular force

Giant covalent structures

Key points

- Covalently bonded substances with giant structures have very high melting points.
- Diamond is a form of carbon whose atoms each form four covalent bonds.
- Graphite is another form of carbon where the carbon atoms form layers that can slide over each other.
- Graphite can conduct electricity because of the delocalised electrons in its structure.
- Carbon also exists as fullerenes.

- Atoms of some elements can form several covalent bonds. These atoms can join together in **giant covalent structures** (sometimes called **macromolecules**). Every atom in the structure is joined to several other atoms by strong covalent bonds. It takes an enormous amount of energy to break down the lattice and so these substances have very high melting points.

▶ **1** *Why do substances with giant covalent structures have very high melting points?*

- Diamond is a form of carbon that has a regular three-dimensional giant structure. Every carbon atom is covalently bonded to four other carbon atoms. This makes diamond hard and transparent. The compound silicon dioxide (silica) has a similar structure.

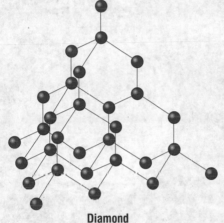

Diamond

Figure 1 Part of the giant structure of diamond

- Graphite is a form of carbon in which each atom is covalently bonded to three other carbon atoms in giant flat two-dimensional layers. There are no covalent bonds between the layers and so they can slide over each other, making graphite slippery and grey.

- In graphite each carbon atom bonds covalently to three other carbon atoms forming a flat sheet of hexagons. One electron from each carbon atom is delocalised, rather like electrons in a metal. These **delocalised electrons** allow graphite to conduct heat and electricity.

- There are only weak intermolecular forces between the layers in graphite, so the layers can slide over each other quite easily.

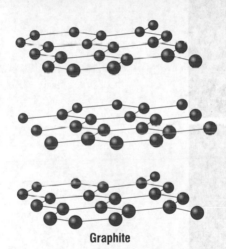

Graphite

Figure 2 Part of the giant structure of graphite. When you write with a pencil, some layers of carbon atoms slide off the 'lead' and are left on the paper.

▶ **2** *Give two similarities and two differences between diamond and graphite.*

- **Fullerenes** are large molecules formed from hexagonal rings of carbon atoms. The rings join together to form cage-like shapes with different numbers of carbon atoms. Some of these structures are nano-sized. Scientists are finding many applications for fullerenes, including drug delivery into the body, lubricants, catalysts and reinforcing materials. (See Figure 1 on page 22.)

▶ **3** *Give two similarities and one difference between graphite and fullerenes.*

Study tip

Diamond and graphite both have very high melting points because they are both giant covalent structures. However you should make sure that you are able to explain the differences in the properties of graphite and diamond in terms of intermolecular forces and delocalised electrons.

Key words: giant covalent structure, macromolecule, delocalised electron, fullerene

Nanoscience

Key points

- Nanoscience is the study of small particles that are between 1 and 100 nanometres in size.

- Nanoparticles behave differently from the bulk materials they are made from.

- Developments in nanoscience are exciting but will need more research into possible issues that might arise from increased use.

∞ **links**

Revise more on the effect of increasing surface area on the rate of reactions in 8.2 'Collision theory and surface area'.

- **Nanoscience** is a new and exciting area of science. When atoms are arranged into very small particles they behave differently to ordinary materials made of the same atoms. A nanometre is one billionth of a metre (or 10^{-9} m) and nanoparticles are a few nanometres in size. They contain a few hundred atoms arranged in a particular way. Their very small sizes give them very large surface areas and new properties that can make them very useful materials.

▶ **1** *What is a nanoparticle?*

- Nanotechnology uses nanoparticles as highly selective sensors, very efficient catalysts, new coatings, new cosmetics such as sun screens and deodorants, and to give construction materials special properties.

Figure 1 Nanocages can carry drugs inside them and nanotubes can reinforce materials

- If nanoparticles are used more and more there will be a greater risk of them finding their way into the air and into our bodies. This could have unpredictable consequences for our health and the environment. More research needs to be done to find out their effects.

▶ **2** *Scientists have developed a new deodorant containing nanoparticles. What should be done before it is sold for people to use?*

Key word: nanoscience

1 **a** Which electrons in an atom are involved in bonding?

b What happens to the electrons in atoms when ionic bonds are formed?

c What happens to electrons in atoms when covalent bonds are formed?

2 **a** Why do the elements in Group 1 form ions with a single positive charge?

b Why do the elements in Group 7 form ions with a single negative charge?

3 Write the correct formula for each of the following: lithium chloride, sodium oxide, calcium fluoride, magnesium hydroxide, sodium sulfate, calcium nitrate.

4 Draw a diagram to show the bonding in methane, CH_4.

5 Draw diagrams using symbols and lines to show the covalent bonds in F_2, O_2, HBr, H_2O, NH_3.

6 Draw diagrams to show what happens when a potassium atom reacts with a fluorine atom.

7 C_{60} is a fullerene. What are fullerenes?

8 Why does it take a lot of energy to melt sodium chloride?

9 Why are compounds such as methane, CH_4, and ammonia, NH_3, gases at room temperature?

10 Why do ionic compounds need to be molten or in solution to conduct electricity?

11 Why can graphite conduct electricity?

12 Explain what is meant by 'intermolecular forces'.

Chapter checklist ✓✓✓

Tick when you have:

reviewed it after your lesson	✓ ☐ ☐
revised once – some questions right	✓ ✓ ☐
revised twice – all questions right	✓ ✓ ✓

Move on to another topic when you have all three ticks

Atoms into ions	☐ ☐ ☐
Ionic bonding	☐ ☐ ☐
Giant ionic structures	☐ ☐ ☐
Covalent bonding	☐ ☐ ☐
Simple molecules	☐ ☐ ☐
Giant covalent structures	☐ ☐ ☐
Nanoscience	☐ ☐ ☐

C4.1

Gases in the atmosphere

Key points

- The main gases in the Earth's atmosphere are nitrogen and oxygen.
- About four-fifths (78%) of the atmosphere is nitrogen, and about one-fifth (21%) is oxygen.
- The main gases in the air can be separated by fractional distillation. These gases are used in industry as useful raw materials.

- The atmosphere is almost four-fifths nitrogen and just over one-fifth oxygen.
- Other gases in the atmosphere include carbon dioxide, water vapour and noble gases. These make up about 1% of the atmosphere.

▌▌▌➡ **1** *What are the approximate percentages of nitrogen and oxygen in the air?*

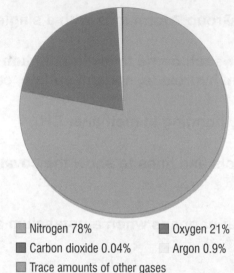

■ Nitrogen 78%　　■ Oxygen 21%
■ Carbon dioxide 0.04%　　■ Argon 0.9%
■ Trace amounts of other gases

Figure 1 The relative proportions of nitrogen, oxygen and other gases in the Earth's atmosphere

Maths skills

Pie charts

Pie charts are a way of presenting data visually. They are useful for showing percentages, where the total (100%) is represented by a complete circle of 360°. Therefore each 1% is represented by 360/100 = 3.6° segments of the circle.

So the percentage of oxygen in the atmosphere (21%) is shown as a (21 × 3.6)° segment i.e. a 75.6° 'slice of the pie'.

Study tip

To get maximum marks, you should be able to explain the fractional distillation of liquid air, given the boiling points of nitrogen and oxygen.

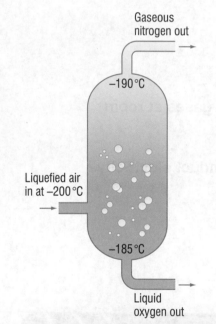

Figure 2 Fractional distillation of liquid air

links

Revise how a fractionating column is used to separate crude oil into fractions in 9.2 'Fractional distillation'.

Key word: fractional distillation

Separating the gases in air

- The gases in the air have different boiling points and so can be separated from liquid air by **fractional distillation**.
- Fractional distillation of liquid air is done industrially to produce pure oxygen and liquid nitrogen, which have important uses.
- The air is cooled to below −200 °C and fed into a fractional distillation column.
- Nitrogen is separated from oxygen and argon and further distillation is used to produce pure oxygen and argon.

▌▌▌➡ **2** *Why can the gases in air be separated by fractional distillation?*

C4.2 Oxygen and oxides

Key points

- Oxygen is the reactive gas in air. It reacts with substances to form oxides.

- Metallic elements form basic oxides. If they dissolve in water, their solutions will be alkaline.

- Non-metallic elements form oxides that dissolve in water to form acidic solutions.

- Amphoteric oxides react like both acids and bases.

- Oxidation can be thought of as the addition of oxygen. The removal of oxygen from a compound is called reduction.

links

Revise the reduction of metal oxides in 7.3 'Extracting metals'.

- The reactive gas in the air is oxygen. When any substance burns, it reacts with the oxygen gas in air to form compounds called oxides.

- The metallic elements burn to form solid oxides. For example:

$$2Mg(s) + O_2(g) \rightarrow 2MgO(s)$$

- When non-metallic elements burn they often form oxides that are produced as gases. For example:

$$C(s) + O_2(g) \rightarrow CO_2(g)$$
$$S(s) + O_2(g) \rightarrow SO_2(g)$$

- These reactions with oxygen to form oxides are known as combustion reactions. They are examples of **oxidation**, in which oxygen is added to an element.

- Other reactions, in which oxygen is removed from an oxide are known as **reduction**. This is important in the extraction of metals from their ores. For example, in the extraction of iron, iron(III) oxide from iron ore is reduced to iron in a blast furnace.

▥▶ **1** *Write a word and symbol equation for the combustion of calcium metal.*

Practical

Testing the pH of oxides

- Collect $2\,cm^3$ of various oxide solutions in separate test tubes.
- Add 3 drops of universal indicator solution to each oxide solution to find its pH.

▥▶ **2** *A solution tested in the experiment had a pH of 14. What will be the colour of the universal indicator solution, and what does this pH indicate?*

In general we can say:
- Metal oxides are basic and non-metal oxides are acidic.
- Some oxides, such as water (H_2O) and carbon monoxide (CO), are neutral.
- Other oxides are **amphoteric**. These oxides behave like both acids and **bases**. They react and dissolve in acids, thus behaving like a base, and also react in alkalis, thus behaving like an acid.
- Examples of amphoteric oxides include lead oxide (PbO) and aluminium oxide (Al_2O_3).

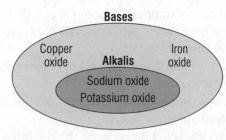

Figure 1 In general, metal oxides are basic and the soluble ones (usually oxides of Group 1 and 2 metals) are alkalis

Key words: oxidation, reduction, amphoteric, base

▥▶ **3 a** *What do we mean by the term amphoteric oxide?*
   b *Name one acidic oxide, one basic oxide and one amphoteric oxide.*

C4.3 Water treatment

Key points

- Water for drinking should contain only low levels of dissolved substances and microbes.
- Water is made fit to drink by passing it through filter beds to remove solids and adding chlorine (sterilising) to reduce the number of microbes.
- We can make pure water by distillation but this requires large amounts of energy which makes it expensive.

- Drinking water should not contain any harmful substances and should have a sufficiently low level of dissolved salts and microbes.
- Water from an appropriate source can be treated to make it safe to drink.
- Water is often treated by sedimentation and filtration to remove solids.
- This is followed by sterilisation (disinfection) to kill microbes in the water. Chlorine is often used to kill microbes in drinking water.

Figure 1 Clean water is a precious resource

▶ **1** *How is water treated to make it fit to drink?*

- We can test for pure water by measuring its boiling point; pure water boils at exactly 100°C.
- Pure water can be produced by distillation. This requires a large amount of energy to boil the water so it would be very expensive to do on a large scale. However, in some countries with few sources of natural freshwater, seawater is converted into usable water for homes and industry. The process is called **desalination.**
- In desalination, seawater undergoes distillation at an industrial plant, but at reduced pressure to lower the boiling point and save energy.
- There are lots of arguments for and against **fluoridation** of public water supplies. For example, dental health improves for some, but people have no choice in taking fluoride if it is in their water supply.
- Some people also choose to use filter jugs in their homes. They pass their water through a filter cartridge. This often contains activated carbon, an ion-exchange resin and silver:
  - The carbon reduces the levels of chlorine left in the water, as well as other organic impurities.
  - The ion-exchange resin removes calcium, magnesium, lead, copper and aluminium ions.
- Silver nanoparticles discourage the growth of bacteria within the filter.

▶ **2** *Give one reason for adding fluorides to water and one reason against.*

Key words: desalination, fluoridation

Study tip

You should know the three main stages in producing water that is fit to drink; a suitable source, the removal of solids and the killing of microbes.

C4.4

Rusting

Key points

- Both air (oxygen) and water are needed for iron to rust.
- Providing a barrier between iron and any air (oxygen) and water protects the iron from rusting.
- Sacrificial protection provides protection against rusting even when the iron is exposed to air and water. The iron needs to be attached to a more reactive metal (either zinc, magnesium or aluminium).

- The corrosion of iron is called **rusting.** Rust is a form of iron(III) oxide called hydrated iron(III) oxide.
- Rusting can be represented as:

iron + oxygen + water → hydrated iron(III) oxide

Practical

What causes iron to rust?
The test tubes are set up as shown below:

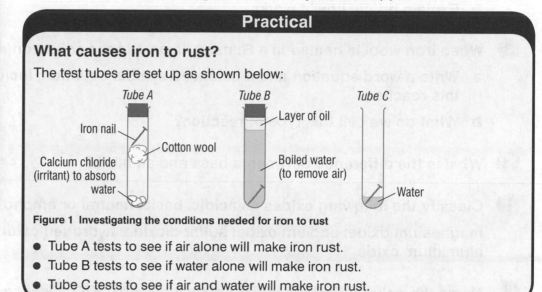

Figure 1 **Investigating the conditions needed for iron to rust**

- Tube A tests to see if air alone will make iron rust.
- Tube B tests to see if water alone will make iron rust.
- Tube C tests to see if air and water will make iron rust.

▉▶ **1** *Why is anhydrous calcium chloride added to tube A in the experiment above?*

- Experiments such as the one above show that the process of rusting needs both air (oxygen) and water to take place.
- Therefore, if we can keep air and water away from iron, it can't rust.
- Methods of preventing rusting include coating the iron with paint, oil, grease, plastic, a less reactive metal or a more reactive metal.
- The last method is called **sacrificial protection** and works even if the coating is scratched and iron is exposed (unlike the other methods).

Practical

How to prevent iron rusting
Set up the test tubes as shown:

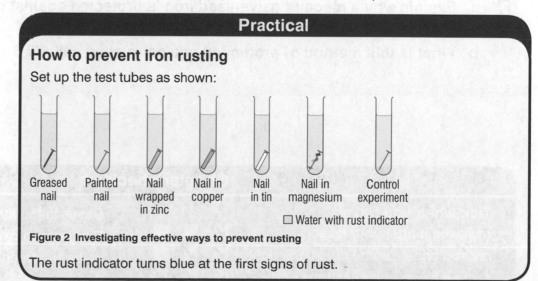

Figure 2 **Investigating effective ways to prevent rusting**

The rust indicator turns blue at the first signs of rust.

Key words: rusting, sacrificial protection

▉▶ **2** *Why is the 'control tube' set up in the experiment above?*

1 Name four gases that are in the atmosphere.

2 **a** Why is the fractional distillation of liquid air done commercially?

b Explain briefly how it works.

3 When iron wool is heated in a Bunsen flame it forms solid iron(III) oxide, Fe_2O_3.

a Write a word equation and a balanced symbol equation, including state symbols for this reaction.

b What do we call this type of reaction?

4 What is the difference between a base and an alkali?

5 Classify the following oxides as acidic, basic, neutral or amphoteric:

magnesium oxide; sodium oxide; sulfur dioxide; hydrogen oxide; carbon dioxide; aluminium oxide

6 Name the solution formed when potassium oxide, K_2O, dissolves and reacts in water.

7 What type of substances are removed from water at a treatment works by filtration?

8 Why is chlorine used in water treatment?

9 Why are fluorides added to water supplies in some areas?

10 What is needed for iron to rust?

11 **a** Explain why a piece of galvanised iron is protected against rusting, even when the thin layer of zinc on its surface gets scratched.

b What is this method of protection against rusting called?

Chapter checklist ✓ ✓ ✓

Tick when you have:

reviewed it after your lesson	✓	☐	☐
revised once – some questions right	✓	✓	☐
revised twice – all questions right	✓	✓	✓

Move on to another topic when you have all three ticks

Gases in the atmosphere	☐	☐	☐
Oxygen and oxides	☐	☐	☐
Water treatment	☐	☐	☐
Rusting	☐	☐	☐

The periodic table

Student Book
pages 56–57

C5.1

Key points

- The atomic (proton) number of an element determines its position in the periodic table.

- The number of electrons in the outermost shell (highest energy level) of an atom determines its chemical properties.

- The group number in the periodic table equals the number of electrons in the outermost shell.

- The noble gases in Group 0 are unreactive because of their very stable electron arrangements.

links

Revise more on electrons in energy levels (or shells) in 1.5 'The arrangement of electrons in atoms'.

- Scientists found out about protons and electrons at the start of the 20th century. Soon after this, they developed models of the arrangement of electrons in atoms. The elements were arranged in the **periodic table** in order of their atomic numbers (proton numbers) and were lined up in vertical **groups**.

- The groups of elements have similar chemical properties because their atoms have the same number of electrons in their highest occupied energy level (outer shell).

- For the main groups in the periodic table: **the number of electrons in the outer shell is the same as the group number.**

▶ **1** *Why do elements in a group have similar chemical properties*

- The atoms of **noble gases** in Group 0 are unreactive because of their very stable electron arrangements. They have 8 electrons in the outermost shell (energy level) except for helium, which has just 2 electrons, but this complete first shell is also a very stable electronic structure.

▶ **2** *Why are the noble gases so unreactive?*

Study tip

Metals react by losing electrons. Non-metals react with metals by gaining electrons.

Key words: periodic table, groups, noble gases

Group numbers																	0
1	2											3	4	5	6	7	4 He 2
7 Li 3	9 Be 4											11 B 5	12 C 6	14 N 7	16 O 8	19 F 9	20 Ne 10
23 Na 11	24 Mg 12											27 Al 13	28 Si 14	31 P 15	32 S 16	35.5 Cl 17	40 Ar 18
39 K 19	40 Ca 20	45 Sc 21	48 Ti 22	51 V 23	52 Cr 24	55 Mn 25	56 Fe 26	59 Co 27	59 Ni 28	63.5 Cu 29	65 Zn 30	70 Ga 31	73 Ge 32	75 As 33	79 Se 34	80 Br 35	84 Kr 36
85 Rb 37	88 Sr 38	89 Y 39	91 Zr 40	93 Nb 41	96 Mo 42	98 Tc 43	101 Ru 44	103 Rh 45	106 Pd 46	108 Ag 47	112 Cd 48	115 In 49	119 Sn 50	122 Sb 51	128 Te 52	127 I 53	131 Xe 54
133 Cs 55	137 Ba 56	139 La 57	178 Hf 72	181 Ta 73	184 W 74	186 Re 75	190 Os 76	192 Ir 77	195 Pt 78	197 Au 79	201 Hg 80	204 Tl 81	207 Pb 82	209 Bi 83	209 Po 84	210 At 85	222 Rn 86
223 Fr 87	226 Ra 88	227 Ac 89															

Relative atomic mass — 1 H — Atomic (proton) number 1

Elements 58–71 and 90–103 (all metals) have been omitted

Key

Reactive metals These metals react vigorously with other elements like oxygen or chlorine, and with water. They are all soft – some of them can even be cut with a knife, like cheese!

Transition elements This group contains the elements that most people probably think of when the word 'metal' is mentioned, like iron, copper, silver and gold. These metals are not usually very reactive – some, like silver and gold, are very unreactive.

Non-metals These elements usually have low melting and boiling points, and many are liquids or gases at room temperature and pressure.

Noble gases These (non-metal) elements are very unreactive, and it is very difficult to get them to combine with other elements.

Figure 1 The modern periodic table

C5.2

Group 1 – the alkali metals

Key points

- The elements in Group 1 of the periodic table are called the alkali metals.
- Their melting points and boiling points decrease going down the group.
- These metals all react with water to produce hydrogen and an alkaline solution containing the metal hydroxide.
- They form positive ions with a charge of 1+ in reactions to make ionic compounds. Their compounds are usually white or colourless crystals that dissolve in water producing colourless solutions.
- The reactivity of the alkali metals increases going down the group.

- The Group 1 elements are called the **alkali metals**. They are all metals that react readily with air and water.
- They are soft solids at room temperature with low melting and boiling points that decrease going down the group. They have low densities, so lithium, sodium and potassium float on water.

Figure 1 We have to store alkali metals in oil

Demonstration

Reactions of alkali metals with water

The reaction of the alkali metals (lithium, sodium and potassium) with water can be demonstrated by dropping a small piece of the metal into a trough of water. This must be done with great care. The reactions are vigorous, releasing a lot of energy. Hydrogen gas is also given off.

Very small piece of alkali metal

Forceps

Trough of water

7	Li	3
23	Na	11
39	K	19
85	Rb	37
133	Cs	55
223	Fr	87

Figure 2 The alkali metals (Group 1)

⃝⃝ links

Revise more about the reactions of metals in 7.1 'The reactivity series'.

Study tip

The alkali metals form only ionic compounds in which their ions have a single positive charge.

▷ **1** *Which of the three alkali metals tested above ignites the hydrogen gas as it is given off in its reaction with water? What colour is the flame?*

- The alkali metals react with water to produce hydrogen gas and a metal hydroxide that is an alkali. For example:

$$\text{sodium} + \text{water} \rightarrow \text{sodium hydroxide} + \text{hydrogen}$$
$$2Na(s) + 2H_2O(l) \rightarrow 2NaOH(aq) + H_2(g)$$

▷ **2** *Why are the elements in Group 1 called 'alkali metals'?*

- They all have one electron in their highest occupied energy level (outer shell). They lose this electron in reactions to form ionic compounds in which their ions have a single positive charge, e.g. Na^+.
- They react with the halogens (Group 7) elements to form salts that are white or colourless crystals. For example:

$$\text{sodium} + \text{chlorine} \rightarrow \text{sodium chloride}$$
$$2Na(s) + Cl_2(g) \rightarrow 2NaCl(s)$$

- Compounds of alkali metals dissolve in water, forming solutions that are usually colourless.
- Going down Group 1, the reactivity of the alkali metals *increases*.

▷ **3** *Name and give the formula of the compound formed when potassium reacts with bromine.*

Key word: alkali metal

C5.3 The transition elements

- The **transition elements** are found in the periodic table between Groups 2 and 3.
- They are all metals and so are sometimes called the **transition metals**.

45 Sc 21	48 Ti 22	51 V 23	52 Cr 24	55 Mn 25	56 Fe 26	59 Co 27	59 Ni 28	63 Cu 29	64 Zn 30
89 Y 39	91 Zr 40	93 Nb 41	96 Mo 42	99 Tc 43	101 Ru 44	103 Rh 45	106 Pd 46	108 Ag 47	112 Cd 48
	178 Hf 72	181 Ta 73	184 W 74	186 Re 75	190 Os 76	192 Ir 77	195 Pt 78	197 Au 79	201 Hg 80

Figure 1 The transition elements. The more common elements are shown in bold type.

Key points

- Compared with the alkali metals, transition elements have much higher melting points and densities. They are also stronger and harder, but are much less reactive.
- The transition elements do not react vigorously with oxygen or water.
- Transition elements can form ions with different charges, in compounds that are often coloured.
- Transition elements and their compounds are important industrial catalysts.

Study tip

For your exam, try to remember how to write formulae for transition metal compounds. The charge on a transition metal ion is given by the Roman numeral in its name. For example, iron(II) chloride contains Fe^{2+} ions and so its formula is $FeCl_2$ and iron(III) chloride contains Fe^{3+} ions and its formula is $FeCl_3$.
You should also be able to balance equations for the reactions of transition metals.

- Except for mercury, the transition elements have higher melting and boiling points than the alkali metals.
- They are malleable and ductile and they are good conductors of heat and electricity.
- They react only slowly, or not at all, with oxygen and water at ordinary temperatures.
- Most are strong and dense and are useful as building materials, often as alloys.

IIII➡ 1 *Why are transition metals useful as building materials?*

- They form positive ions with various charges, e.g. Fe^{2+} and Fe^{3+}.
- Compounds of transition metals are often brightly coloured.
- Many transition metals and their compounds are catalysts for chemical reactions.

IIII➡ 2 *List the ways in which transition elements are different from the elements in Group 1.*

Figure 2 Transition metals are used as building materials, e.g. iron is used in the steel in this bridge

Key words: transition element, transition metal

C5.4

Group 7 – the halogens

Key points

- The **halogens** all form ions with a single negative charge in their ionic compounds with metals.
- The halogens form covalent compounds by sharing electrons with other non-metals.
- A more reactive halogen can displace a less reactive halogen from a solution of one of its salts.
- The reactivity of the halogens decreases going down the group.

Study tip

Make sure you revise ionic and covalent bonding so you are clear about the differences in properties between ionic compounds and covalent compounds that have small molecules (see Chapter 3).

- The **halogens** are non-metallic elements in Group 7 of the periodic table.
- They exist as small molecules made up of pairs of atoms, e.g. Cl_2. There is a single covalent bond between the halogen atoms in their molecules, $Cl—Cl$.
- The halogens have low melting and boiling points that increase going down the group. At room temperature fluorine is a pale yellow gas, chlorine is a green gas, bromine is a red-brown liquid and iodine is a grey solid. Iodine easily vaporises to a violet gas.
- They are all poor conductors of heat and electricity.

Figure 1 Chlorine, bromine and iodine

▶ **1** *Why do the halogens have low melting and boiling points?*

- All of the halogens have seven electrons in their highest occupied energy level.
- The halogens form ionic compounds with metals in which the **halide ions** have a charge of 1–.
- The halogens also bond covalently with non-metals, forming molecules.
- The reactivity of the halogens decreases going down the group.
- A more reactive halogen is able to displace a less reactive halogen from an aqueous solution of a halide compound.
  For example:

$$\text{chlorine } + \text{ potassium iodide} \rightarrow \text{potassium chloride } + \text{ iodine}$$
$$Cl_2(aq) + 2KI(aq) \rightarrow 2KCl(aq) + I_2(aq)$$

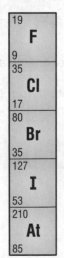

Figure 2 The Group 7 elements, the halogens

Key words: halogens, halide ions

Practical

Displacement reactions

Bromine water is added to potassium iodide solution in a test tube. There are signs of a reaction as the iodine is displaced from its solution.

Other pairs of halogens and halide solutions can also be tested to compare relative reactivity. Signs of a reaction indicate that the halogen added in solution as the element is more reactive than the halogen present in the halide solution.

▶ **2** *How could you show that chlorine is more reactive than bromine?*

C5.5

Explaining trends

Key points

- We can explain trends in reactivity as we go down a group in terms of the attraction between electrons in the outermost shell and the nucleus.

- This electrostatic attraction depends on:
  - the distance between the outermost electrons and the nucleus
  - the number of occupied inner shells (energy levels) of electrons in the atoms.

- These two factors outweigh the increased nuclear charge, due to extra protons in the nucleus, going down a group when deciding how easy it is for atoms to lose or gain electrons from their outermost shell.

∞ links

Revise more about the transfer of electrons between metal and non-metal atoms in 3.1 'Atoms into ions'.

Study tip

For top grades you should be able to explain the trend in reactivity in the main groups in the periodic table in terms of electronic structure.

You may describe electron arrangements in terms of energy levels or shells. The term 'outer electrons' is generally accepted as referring to the electrons in the highest occupied energy level or outer shell.

Reactivity within groups

- Within a group the reactivity of the elements depends on the total number of electrons. Going down a group, there are more occupied energy levels and the atoms get larger. As the atoms get larger, the electrons in the highest occupied energy level (outer shell) are less strongly attracted by the nucleus.

- When metals react they lose electrons, so the reactivity of metals in a group increases going down the group.

- When non-metals react they gain electrons, so the reactivity of non-metals decreases going down a group.

▐▐▐▶ **1** *Why do metals get more reactive going down a group?*

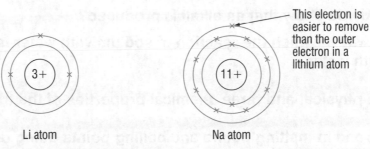

Figure 1 Sodium's outer electron is further from the nuclear charge and is shielded by more inner shell electrons than lithium's outer electron

Explanation of reactivity trend in Group 1

- Reactivity increases going down Group 1 because the outer electron is less strongly attracted to the nucleus as the number of occupied energy levels increases and the atoms get larger.

▐▐▐▶ **2** *Why is lithium less reactive than sodium?*

Explanation of reactivity trend for Group 7

- Reactivity decreases going down Group 7 because the attraction of the outer electrons to the nucleus is less as the number of occupied energy levels (shells) increases.

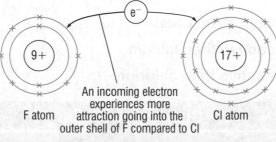

Figure 2 F forms F⁻ more readily than Cl forms Cl⁻

1 How are elements arranged in the periodic table?

2 What is the general name for the unreactive elements found in Group 0 of the periodic table?

3 Why do groups of elements in the periodic table have similar properties?

4 A small piece of lithium is added to a bowl of water.

  a Write a word equation for the reaction of lithium with water.

  b Describe three things that you would see when the lithium is added to the water.

  c How could you show that an alkali is produced?

  d Give one way in which the reaction of sodium with water is different to the reaction of lithium with water.

5 Predict three physical and three chemical properties of the transition element cobalt, Co.

6 What is the trend in melting points and boiling points going down Group 7?

7 What is the formula of sodium bromide? Describe its appearance and what happens when it is mixed with water.

8 Chlorine is a gas at room temperature. Explain why.

9 Some chlorine water was added to an aqueous solution of potassium bromide.

  a Describe the colour change that you would see.

  b Write a word equation for the reaction that happens.

  c Write a balanced symbol equation for the reaction.

10 Iron reacts with chlorine to produce iron(III) chloride. Write a balanced symbol equation for this reaction.

11 Explain in terms of electronic structures:

  a why sodium is more reactive than lithium

  b why fluorine is more reactive than chlorine.

Chapter checklist	✓ ✓ ✓
Tick when you have:	
reviewed it after your lesson ☑ ☐ ☐	The periodic table ☐ ☐ ☐
revised once – some questions right ☑ ☑ ☐	Group 1 – the alkali metals ☐ ☐ ☐
revised twice – all questions right ☑ ☑ ☑	The transition elements ☐ ☐ ☐
Move on to another topic when you have all three ticks	Group 7 – the halogens ☐ ☐ ☐
	Explaining trends ☐ ☐ ☐

1 Magnesium (atomic number 12) is in Group 2 of the periodic table, and fluorine (atomic number 9) is in Group 7.

   a i   Fluorine is a very reactive gas, made up of F_2 molecules. Draw a diagram to show the bonding between the two fluorine atoms in a molecule of fluorine gas. *(2 marks)*

      ii What do we call the type of bonding between the fluorine atoms in a fluorine molecule? *(1 mark)*

   b i   When magnesium bonds to fluorine in magnesium fluoride it involves electron transfer to form ions. Draw a diagram to show the arrangement of electrons in each type of ion formed. *(2 marks)*

      ii Use the periodic table to identify the atoms with the same electron arrangement as the ions drawn in part **i**. *(1 mark)*

      iii Write the chemical formula of each ion drawn in part **i**. *(2 marks)*

      iv Write the chemical formula of magnesium fluoride. *(1 mark)*

      v   What do we call the type of structure in magnesium fluoride? *(1 mark)*

   c The melting point of magnesium fluoride is above 1200 °C whereas fluorine's melting point is –220 °C. Explain fully, in terms of their structures, why there is such a large difference in the melting points of the two substances. *(5 marks)*

   d Fluorine is more reactive than chlorine (atomic number 17).

      i   Explain what you would expect to observe if chlorine gas is bubbled through a solution of sodium fluoride. *(2 marks)*

      ii Write a word equation for the reaction of bromine water with potassium iodide solution. *(1 mark)*

      iii What do we call this type of reaction? *(1 mark)*

      iv Explain the difference in reactivity between fluorine and chlorine, referring to their atomic structures. *(4 marks)*

   e i   Why is chlorine added to water in treatment plants for domestic supplies? *(1 mark)*

      ii Why is fluoride added to water in some areas? *(1 mark)*

      iii Give one argument against the addition of fluoride to domestic water supplies. *(1 mark)*

2 Lithium (atomic number 3), sodium (atomic number 11) and potassium (atomic number 19) are the first three elements in Group 1 of the periodic table.

   a What is an element? *(1 mark)*

   b What is the general name given to the elements in Group 1? *(1 mark)*

   c Lithium reacts with bromine from Group 7.

      i   Name the compound formed. *(1 mark)*

      ii Write the chemical formula of the compound and the ions it contains. *(3 marks)*

      iii Make predictions about the compound by copying and completing the table below:

Colour of compound	Solubility of compound in water (high or low?)	Melting point of compound (high or low?)

      (2 marks)

3 a Sodium reacts with water.

      i   Name the solution formed in the reaction. *(1 mark)*

      ii Name the gas given off. *(1 mark)*

      iii Describe the positive test for the gas given off. *(1 mark)*

      iv Write a balanced symbol equation, including state symbols, for the reaction of sodium with water. *(3 marks)*

   b Explain why potassium is a more reactive element than sodium. Refer to the atomic structures of the atoms in your answer. *(4 marks)*

Study tip

When writing the formula of an iconic compound, the charges on the ions must cancel out as the compound carries no overall charge. For example, aluminium ions, Al^{3+}, and oxide ions, O^{2-}, combine in the ratio 2 : 3 so the formula of aluminium oxide is Al_2O_3.

Study tip

When asked how to test for a particular gas, always describe how to do the test **and** the result of the test.

Acids and alkalis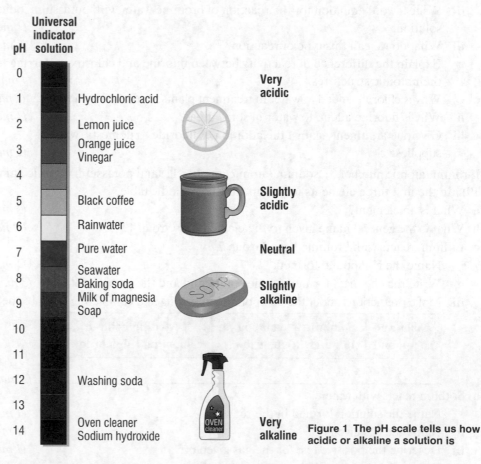

- Pure water is **neutral** and has a pH value of 7.
- **Acids** are substances that produce hydrogen ions, H⁺(aq), when they are added to water.
- When we dissolve a substance in water we make an **aqueous solution**.
- The state symbol (aq) shows that the ions are in aqueous solution. Hydrogen ions make solutions acidic and they have pH values of less than 7.

> **1** *Which ions are produced by acids when they are added to water?*

- **Bases** react with acids and neutralise them.
- **Alkalis** are bases that dissolve in water to make alkaline solutions. Alkalis produce hydroxide ions, OH⁻(aq), in the solution. Alkaline solutions have pH values greater than 7.

> **2** *What is an alkali?*

- The **pH scale** has values from 0 to 14. Solutions that are very acidic have low pH values of between 0 and 2. Solutions that are very alkaline have high pH values of 12 to 14.
- Indicators have different colours in acidic and alkaline solutions. **Universal indicator** (**UI**) and full-range indicators have different colours at different pH values.

Key points

- When acids are added to water they produce hydrogen ions, H⁺(aq), in the solution.
- Bases are substances that will neutralise acids.
- Alkalis dissolve in water to give hydroxide ions, OH⁻(aq), in the solution.
- The pH scale shows how acidic or alkaline a solution is.

Study tip

All alkalis are bases, and all bases neutralise acids, but only bases that dissolve in water are alkalis.

Maths skills

Using mathematical symbols

We can use the mathematical symbols ' > ' (read as 'is greater than') and ' < ' ('is less than') when interpreting pH values.

We can say:

pH < 7 indicates an acidic solution.

i.e. pH values less than 7 are acidic.

pH > 7 indicates an alkaline solution.

i.e. pH values greater than 7 are alkaline.

Figure 1 The pH scale tells us how acidic or alkaline a solution is

Key words: neutral, acid, aqueous solution, base, alkali, pH scale, universal indicator (UI)

> **3** *Which indicators can tell us the pH of a solution?*

C6.2

Making salts from metals or insoluble bases

Key points

- A salt is a compound formed when the hydrogen in an acid is wholly or partially replaced by metal or ammonium ions.

- When we react an acid with a base, a neutralisation reaction occurs.

- The reaction between an acid and a base produces a salt and water.

- Salts can also be made by reacting a suitable metal with an acid. This reaction produces hydrogen gas as well as a salt. A sample of the salt made can then be crystallised out of solution by evaporating off the water.

⊙ links

Revise more on neutralisation reactions between metal oxides and acids in 4.2 'Oxygen and oxides'.

Study tip

Learn the formulae of the three important acids HCl, HNO_3 and H_2SO_4 to help you to write the formulae of their salts. Remember that when they form salts hydrogen is lost from the acid so they form chlorides, nitrates and sulfates.

➤ 2 *Why do we add excess of the base when making a salt?*

Key words: salt, neutralisation

- Acids will react with metals that are above hydrogen in the reactivity series.
- However, the reactions of acids with very reactive metals, such as sodium and potassium, are too violent to be done safely.
- When metals react with acids they produce a **salt** and hydrogen gas.

$$\text{acid} + \text{metal} \rightarrow \text{a salt} + \text{hydrogen}$$
$$H_2SO_4(aq) + Zn(s) \rightarrow ZnSO_4(aq) + H_2(g)$$

➤ 1 *Name a metal other than zinc that can safely react with an acid to produce a salt.*

- Metal oxides and metal hydroxides are bases. When an acid reacts with a base a **neutralisation** reaction takes place and a salt and water are produced.

$$\text{acid} + \text{base} \rightarrow \text{a salt} + \text{water}$$
$$2HCl(aq) + MgO(s) \rightarrow MgCl_2(aq) + H_2O(l)$$

- These reactions can be used to make salts. Chlorides are made from hydrochloric acid, nitrates from nitric acid and sulfates from sulfuric acid.
- We can add a metal, or a base that is insoluble in water, a little at a time to the acid until all of the acid has reacted. The mixture is then filtered to remove the excess solid reactant, leaving a solution of the salt. The solid salt is made when water is evaporated from the solution so that it crystallises.

Practical

Making a copper salt

Crystals of copper(II) sulfate can be made from copper oxide (an insoluble base) and dilute sulfuric acid.

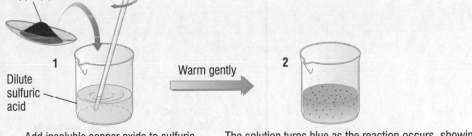

Add insoluble copper oxide to sulfuric acid and stir. Warm gently on a tripod and gauze (do not boil).

The solution turns blue as the reaction occurs, showing that copper sulfate is being formed. Excess black copper oxide can be seen.

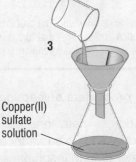

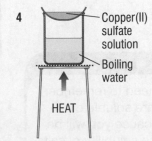

When the reaction is complete, filter the solution to remove excess copper oxide

We can evaporate the water so that crystals of copper sulfate start to form. Stop heating when you see the first crystals appear at the edge of the solution. Then leave for the rest of the water to evaporate off slowly. This will give you larger crystals.

Student Book
pages 72–73 **C6.3**

Neutralisation, precipitation and making salts

Key points

- An indicator is needed when a soluble salt is prepared by reacting an alkali with an acid.
- Insoluble salts can be made by reacting two solutions to produce a precipitate.
- Precipitation is an important way of removing some metal ions from industrial wastewater.

⬭⬭ links

To revise the use of precipitation reactions to identify metal ions, see 15.1 'Tests for positive ions'.

- We can make soluble salts by reacting an acid and an alkali: e.g.

$$acid + alkali \rightarrow salt + water$$
$$HCl(aq) + NaOH(aq) \rightarrow NaCl(aq) + H_2O(l)$$

- We can represent the neutralisation reaction between any acid and any alkali by this ionic equation:

$$H^+(aq) + OH^-(aq) \rightarrow H_2O(l)$$

- There is no visible change when acids react with alkalis so we need to use an indicator or a pH meter to show when the reaction is complete. The solid salt can be obtained from the solution by crystallisation.

▐▐▐➡ **1** *What compound is produced in every neutralisation reaction?*

- Ammonia solution is an alkali that does not contain a metal. It reacts with acids to produce ammonium salts, such as ammonium nitrate, NH_4NO_3. Ammonium salts are used as fertilisers.

- We can make **insoluble salts** by mixing solutions of soluble salts that contain the ions needed. For example, we can make lead iodide by mixing solutions of lead nitrate and potassium iodide. The lead iodide forms a **precipitate** that can be filtered from the solution, washed with distilled water and dried.

$$Pb(NO_3)_2(aq) + 2KI(aq) \rightarrow PbI_2(s) + 2KNO_3(aq)$$

Practical

Making an insoluble salt

The salt lead iodide can be made from lead nitrate solution and potassium iodide solution. The equation for the reaction is shown above.

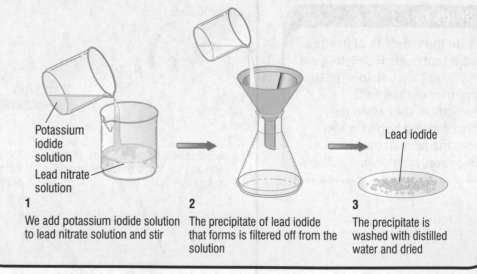

Potassium iodide solution
Lead nitrate solution

1 We add potassium iodide solution to lead nitrate solution and stir

2 The precipitate of lead iodide that forms is filtered off from the solution

Lead iodide

3 The precipitate is washed with distilled water and dried

▐▐▐➡ **2** *Why is the precipitate of lead iodide washed with distilled water?*

- Some pollutants, such as metal ions, can be removed from water by precipitation. The water is treated by adding substances that react with the pollutant metal ions dissolved in the water to form insoluble salts.

▐▐▐➡ **3** *Zinc carbonate is insoluble in water. What would happen when sodium carbonate solution is added to zinc sulfate solution?*

Study tip

You do not need to remember which salts are soluble or insoluble because you will be told about the solubility of salts in any exam questions.

Key word: precipitate

C6.4 Metal carbonates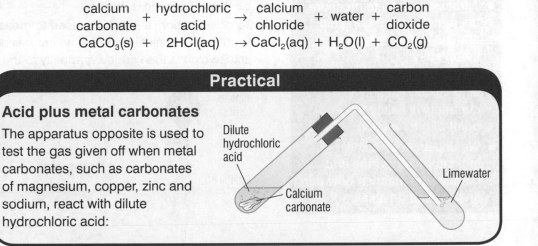

Key points

- Carbonates react with dilute acid to form a salt, water and carbon dioxide.

- Limewater turns cloudy in the test for carbon dioxide gas. A precipitate of insoluble calcium carbonate causes the cloudiness.

- Metal carbonates decompose on heating to form the metal oxide and carbon dioxide.

- Limestone, containing mainly calcium carbonate ($CaCO_3$), is quarried and can be used as a building material, or powdered and used to control acidity in the soil. It can also be used in the manufacture of cement, glass and iron, as well as producing calcium oxide (lime) when heated.

- All carbonates react with acids to produce a salt, water and carbon dioxide gas. For example:

$$\text{calcium carbonate} + \text{hydrochloric acid} \rightarrow \text{calcium chloride} + \text{water} + \text{carbon dioxide}$$

$$CaCO_3(s) + 2HCl(aq) \rightarrow CaCl_2(aq) + H_2O(l) + CO_2(g)$$

Practical

Acid plus metal carbonates

The apparatus opposite is used to test the gas given off when metal carbonates, such as carbonates of magnesium, copper, zinc and sodium, react with dilute hydrochloric acid:

▷ **1** *What conclusion can you draw from this experiment?*

- Limestone (which is mainly calcium carbonate) is damaged by acid rain because the calcium carbonate in the limestone reacts with acids in the rain.

- Calcium hydroxide solution is called **limewater**. Limewater is used to test for carbon dioxide. The limewater turns cloudy because it reacts with carbon dioxide to produce insoluble calcium carbonate.
  The reaction is:

$$\text{calcium hydroxide} + \text{carbon dioxide} \rightarrow \text{calcium carbonate} + \text{water}$$
$$\text{(limewater)} \qquad\qquad\qquad \text{(an insoluble white precipitate)}$$
$$Ca(OH)_2(aq) + CO_2(g) \rightarrow CaCO_3(s) + H_2O(l)$$

▷ **2** *Write a word equation and a balanced symbol equation, including state symbols, for the reaction of magnesium carbonate with dilute hydrochloric acid.*

- All metal carbonates react in similar ways when heated.

- Metal carbonates decompose to the metal oxide and carbon dioxide when they are heated strongly enough.

$$CaCO_3(s) \rightarrow CaO(s) + CO_2(g)$$
$$\text{(lime or quicklime)}$$

This type of reaction is called **thermal decomposition**.

- Note that a Bunsen burner flame cannot get hot enough to decompose sodium carbonate or potassium carbonate.

▷ **3** *What are the products when zinc carbonate is heated strongly?*

Study tip

Thermal decomposition means 'breaking down by heating'. You need to make both points – 'breaking down' and 'by heating' – to get full marks.

Key words: limewater, thermal decomposition

C6.5

Titrations

Student Book pages 76–77

Key points

- Titration is used to measure accurately how much acid and alkali react together completely.

- The point at which an acid–alkali reaction is complete is called the end point of the reaction.

- We use an acid–alkali indicator to show the end point of the reaction between an acid and an alkali.

- When solutions of an acid and an alkali react to form a salt and water, a neutralisation reaction takes place. The volumes of solutions that react exactly can be found by using a **titration**.

- To do a titration, a **pipette** is used to measure accurately the volume of alkali that is put into a conical flask. An indicator is added to the alkali. A **burette** is filled with acid, which is then added gradually to the flask.

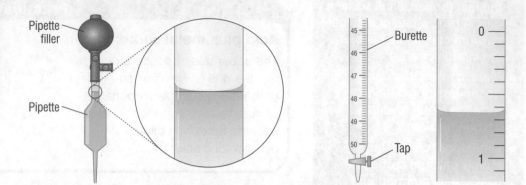

Figure 1 A pipette with a pipette filler attached and a burette

links

Revise more on neutralisation reactions in 6.2 'Making salts from metals or bases' and 6.3 'Neutralisation, precipitation and making salts'.

 **1** *What is the difference between a pipette and a burette?*

- When the indicator changes colour, the **end point** has been reached. The volume of acid used is found from the initial and final burette readings.
- You should do the titration several times to improve the repeatability of the results.

Practical

Carrying out a titration

This titration is used to find out how much acid is needed to completely react with an alkali:

Study tip

Make sure you can describe how to use a pipette and a burette to do a titration and obtain results that are precise and repeatable.

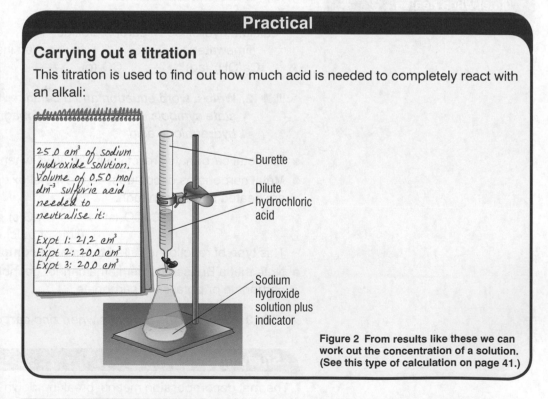

25.0 cm³ of sodium hydroxide solution. Volume of 0.50 mol dm⁻³ sulfuric acid needed to neutralise it:

Expt 1: 21.2 cm³
Expt 2: 20.0 cm³
Expt 3: 20.0 cm³

Burette

Dilute hydrochloric acid

Sodium hydroxide solution plus indicator

Figure 2 From results like these we can work out the concentration of a solution. (See this type of calculation on page 41.)

Figure 3 Titration experiment

2 *Why is an indicator needed in acid–alkali titrations?*

Key words: titration, pipette, burette, end point

C6.6 # Titration calculations

Key points

- To calculate the concentration of a solution, given the mass of solute in a certain volume:
  1 Calculate the mass (in grams) of solute in 1 cm^3 of solution.
  2 Calculate the mass (in grams) of solute in 1000 cm^3 of solution.
  3 Convert the mass (in grams) to moles.

- To calculate the mass of solute in a certain volume of solution of known concentration:
  1 Calculate the mass (in grams) of the solute there is in 1 dm^3 (1000 cm^3) of solution.
  2 Calculate the mass (in grams) of solute in 1 cm^3 of solution.
  3 Calculate the mass (in grams) of solute there is in the given volume of the solution.

Study tip

To get the highest grades in your exam, you should be able to balance symbol equations for reactions, calculate amounts of substances from titration results and apply these skills to solving problems.

Maths skills

Remember this equation for calculations:

number of moles =
$$\frac{\text{mass in grams}}{\text{relative formula mass}}$$

⬭⬭ links

To revise more about moles and calculations using chemical equations look back at 2.4 'Equations and calculations'.

Concentrations and titration calculations

- Concentrations of solutions are measured in grams per decimetre cubed (g/dm^3) or moles per decimetre cubed (mol/dm^3).
- If we know the mass or the number of moles of a substance dissolved in a given volume of solution we can calculate its concentration.
- If we know the volume of a solution and its concentration we can calculate the mass or the number of moles of the substance in any volume of solution.

Worked examples

a 50 cm^3 solution was made using 5.6 g of potassium hydroxide, KOH. What is its concentration in g/dm^3 and mol/dm^3?

1 cm^3 of solution contains (5.6/50) g so 1 dm^3 of solution contains
(5.6/50) × 1000 g = 112 g
concentration of solution = **112 g/dm^3**
1 mole KOH = (39 + 16 + 1) g = 56 g
112 g /56 g = 2 mole; therefore concentration of solution = **2 mol/dm^3**

b What is the mass of sodium hydroxide in 100 cm^3 of a solution with a concentration of 0.2 mol/dm^3?
100 cm^3 contains 100 × 0.2/1000 mol = 0.02 mol
1 mol NaOH = 40 g; therefore 0.02 mol has a mass of 0.02 × 40 = **8 g**

> ⓲⟹ **1** *100 cm^3 of solution was made using 1.2 g LiOH. What is its concentration in g/dm^3 and mol/dm^3? (Relative atomic masses: Li = 7, O = 16, H = 1)*

- Titrations are used to find the volumes of solutions that react exactly.
- If the concentration of one of the solutions is known, and the volumes that react together are known, the concentration of the other solution can be calculated. This information can be used to find the amount of a substance in a sample.
- The concentrations are calculated using balanced symbol equations and moles.

Worked example

A student found that 25.0 cm^3 of sodium hydroxide solution with an unknown concentration reacted with exactly 20.0 cm^3 of 0.50 mol/dm^3 hydrochloric acid. What was the concentration of the sodium hydroxide solution?

The balanced symbol equation for this reaction is:

$$NaOH(aq) + HCl(aq) \rightarrow NaCl(aq) + H_2O(l)$$

The concentration of the HCl is 0.50 mol/dm^3, so 0.50 mol of HCl are dissolved in 1000 cm^3 of acid.

Therefore 20.0 cm^3 of acid contains 20 × 0.50/1000 mol = 0.010 mol HCl

The equation for the reaction tells us that 0.010 mol of HCl will react with exactly 0.010 mol of NaOH.

This means that there must have been 0.010 mol of NaOH in the 25.0 cm^3 of solution in the conical flask.

So, the concentration of NaOH solution = (0.010/25) × 1000 = **0.40 mol/dm^3**

> ⓲⟹ **2** *15.0 cm^3 of hydrochloric acid reacted exactly with 25.0 cm^3 of sodium hydroxide solution that had a concentration of 0.10 mol/dm^3. What was the concentration of the hydrochloric acid in mol/dm^3?*

1 Dilute nitric acid is added to sodium hydroxide solution.

  a What type of substance is sodium hydroxide?

  b What type of reaction happens?

  c Why is an indicator used to show when the reaction is complete?

  d Write a word equation for the reaction.

2 Describe the main steps to make zinc sulfate crystals from zinc oxide and dilute sulfuric acid.

3 Describe how you could make some insoluble lead sulfate from solutions of lead nitrate and sodium sulfate.

4 What is meant by 'thermal decomposition' of a compound?

5 Name the products formed when calcium carbonate is heated strongly.

6 Limewater goes cloudy when mixed with carbon dioxide. Explain why, using an equation in your answer.

7 Explain, as fully as you can, why acids damage limestone.

8 Farmers spread calcium hydroxide on fields with acidic soils. Explain why, naming the type of reaction that takes place and the property of calcium hydroxide on which this reaction depends.

9 Balance this symbol equation:

$$K_2CO_3 + HCl \rightarrow KCl + H_2O + CO_2$$

10 12.5 cm³ of 0.10 mol/dm³ hydrochloric acid reacted exactly with 25.0 cm³ of potassium hydroxide solution. What was the concentration in mol/dm³ of the potassium hydroxide solution?

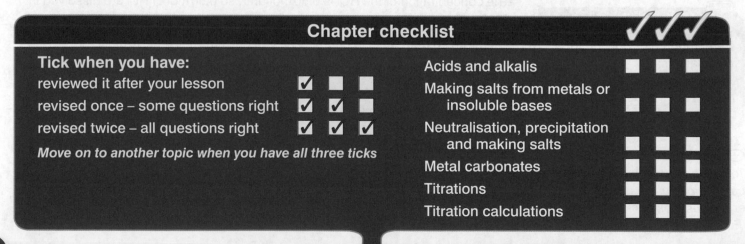

Chapter checklist ✓✓✓

Tick when you have:

reviewed it after your lesson	✓	☐	☐
revised once – some questions right	✓	✓	☐
revised twice – all questions right	✓	✓	✓

Move on to another topic when you have all three ticks

Acids and alkalis	☐	☐	☐
Making salts from metals or insoluble bases	☐	☐	☐
Neutralisation, precipitation and making salts	☐	☐	☐
Metal carbonates	☐	☐	☐
Titrations	☐	☐	☐
Titration calculations	☐	☐	☐

C7.1

The reactivity series

- Metals can be placed in order of reactivity by their reactions with water and dilute acid.
- Hydrogen gas is given off if metals react with water or dilute acids. The gas 'pops' with a lighted splint.

- Most metals are found as compounds in rocks. Rock that contains enough of a metal or a metal compound to make it economically worthwhile extracting the metal is called an **ore**.
- The **reactivity series** is a list of metals in order of their reactivity, with the most reactive metals at the top and the least reactive ones at the bottom.
- The Group 1 metals react vigorously with water, giving off hydrogen gas and leaving alkaline hydroxide solutions. For example:

potassium + water → potassium hydroxide + hydrogen
$$2K(s) + 2H_2O(l) → 2KOH(aq) + H_2(g)$$

- Magnesium metal reacts very slowly with cold water, but we can speed up the reaction by heating and reacting the metal with steam. The reaction can be demonstrated as shown below:

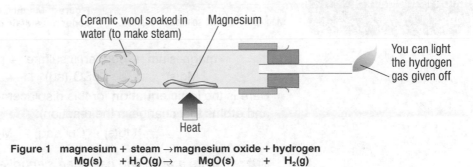

Ceramic wool soaked in water (to make steam)   Magnesium

You can light the hydrogen gas given off

Heat

Figure 1   magnesium + steam → magnesium oxide + hydrogen
$$Mg(s) + H_2O(g) → MgO(s) + H_2(g)$$

> **1** *Which gas can be burnt off at the end of the tube when magnesium is reacting with steam?*

- The rate at which the metal gives off hydrogen gas can be used to judge the relative reactivity of magnesium, zinc, iron, tin and lead.
- When a lighted splint is applied to hydrogen, it burns with a squeaky 'pop'.

The reactivity series of metals

> **2 a** *When comparing the reactivity of metals with dilute acid, name two variables that should be controlled to make it a fair test?*
> **b** *Why is it often difficult to carry out a fair test between different metals and dilute acid?*

Order of reactivity	Reaction with water	Reaction with dilute acid
potassium	fizz, giving off hydrogen, leaving an alkaline solution of metal hydroxide	explode
sodium		
lithium		
calcium		fizz, giving off hydrogen and forming a salt
magnesium	react with steam, giving off hydrogen and forming the metal oxide	
aluminium		
zinc		
iron		
tin	slight reaction with steam	react slowly with warm acid
lead		
copper	no reaction, even with steam	no reaction
silver		
gold		

⬭ links

Revise more about the reaction of metals with dilute acid in 6.2 'Making salts from metals or insoluble bases'.

Key words: ore, reactivity series

Note: Aluminium is protected by a layer of aluminium oxide so will not undergo the reactions above unless the oxide layer is removed.

C7.2 # Displacement reactions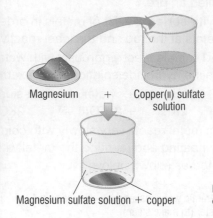

Key points

- A more reactive metal will displace a less reactive metal from its aqueous solution.

- The non-metals hydrogen and carbon can be given positions in the reactivity series on the basis of displacement reactions.

- Oxidation is the loss of electrons.

- Reduction is the gain of electrons.

● A more reactive metal will displace a less reactive metal from its aqueous solution. For example, look at the **displacement reaction** below:

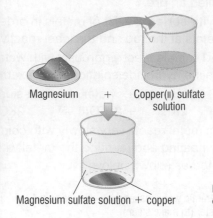

Magnesium + Copper(II) sulfate solution

Magnesium sulfate solution + copper

Figure 1 Magnesium displaces copper from copper(II) sulfate solution

$$\text{magnesium} + \text{copper(II) sulfate} \rightarrow \text{magnesium sulfate} + \text{copper}$$
$$Mg(s) + CuSO_4(aq) \rightarrow MgSO_4(aq) + Cu(s)$$

● Here is the **ionic equation** for this displacement reaction (showing only the ions and atoms that change in the reaction):

$$Mg(s) + Cu^{2+}(aq) \rightarrow Mg^{2+}(aq) + Cu(s)$$

> **1** *Write a word and balanced symbol equation, including state symbols, for the reaction between zinc granules and copper(II) sulfate solution.*

● The non-metals hydrogen and carbon can be included in the reactivity series by using displacement reactions. Hydrogen is positioned between copper and lead. Carbon is placed between aluminium and zinc in the series.

> **2** *Place the following five elements in order of reactivity, with the most reactive first:*
>
> *hydrogen; magnesium; copper; iron; carbon*

● **Oxidation** can be defined as the loss of electrons.
● **Reduction** can be defined as the gain of electrons.
● The displacement reaction between zinc and copper(II) sulfate can be used to explain a redox (reduction–oxidation) reaction:

Ionic equation: $Zn(s) + Cu^{2+}(aq) \rightarrow Zn^{2+}(aq) + Cu(s)$

What happens to each reactant in the ionic equation?

$$Zn(s) \rightarrow Zn^{2+}(aq) + 2e^-$$

Zinc atoms lose two electrons to form zinc ions. This is oxidation (the loss of electrons). We say that zinc atoms have been oxidised.

These two electrons from zinc are gained by the copper(II) ions as they form copper atoms:

$$Cu^{2+}(aq) + 2e^- \rightarrow Cu(s)$$

This is reduction (the gain of electrons). The copper(II) ions have been reduced.

> **3** *In the displacement reaction between magnesium atoms and copper(II) ions in solution, which reactant is oxidised and which is reduced?*

Study tip

You can use 'OIL-RIG' to help you remember the definition of reduction and oxidation in terms of electron transfer: 'Oxidation Is Loss; Reduction Is Gain'

Key words: displacement reaction, ionic equation, oxidation, reduction

Student Book
pages 86–87

C7.3

Extracting metals

Key points

- Ores are mined from the ground and might need to be concentrated before the metal is extracted and purified.

- We can find gold and other unreactive metals in their native state.

- The reactivity series helps us decide the best way to extract a metal from its ore. The oxides of metals below carbon in the series can be reduced by carbon to give the metal element.

- Metals more reactive than carbon cannot be extracted from their ores using carbon. They are extracted by electrolysing the molten metal compound.

links

Revise the use of electrolysis to extract reactive metals in 14.3 'The extraction of aluminium'.

Study tip

You should be able to write a balanced symbol equation for the reduction of a named metal oxide by carbon.

Key words: reactivity series, reduction, electrolysis

- Mining ores often involves digging up large amounts of rock. The ore may need to be concentrated before the metal is extracted. These processes can produce large amounts of waste and may have major impacts on the environment.
- Whether it is worth extracting a particular metal depends on:
  – how easy it is to extract it from its ore
  – how much metal the ore contains.

Figure 1 An open-cast copper mine scars the landscape

1 *What is an ore?*

- A few unreactive metals, low in the **reactivity series**, such as gold are found in the Earth as the metal. Gold can be separated from rocks by physical methods.
- However, most metals are found as compounds. So then the metals have to be extracted by chemical reactions.
- Metals can be extracted from compounds by displacement using a more reactive element.
- Metals which are less reactive than carbon can be extracted from their oxides by heating with carbon. A **reduction** reaction takes place as carbon removes the oxygen from the oxide to produce the metal. This method is used commercially if possible. For example:

$$\text{lead(II) oxide} + \text{carbon} \xrightarrow{\text{heat}} \text{lead} + \text{carbon dioxide}$$
$$2PbO(s) + C(s) \longrightarrow 2Pb(l) + CO_2(g)$$

2 a *Name two metals that have oxides that can be reduced by carbon?*
  b *What do we call the removal of oxygen from a metal oxide?*

- The metals that are more reactive than carbon are not extracted from their ores by reduction with carbon. Instead they are extracted by **electrolysis** of the molten metal compound (see Chapter 14).

C7.4 **Extracting copper**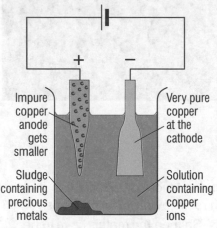

Key points

- Most copper is extracted by smelting (roasting) copper-rich ores, although our limited supplies of ores are becoming scarcer.

- Copper can be extracted from copper solutions by electrolysis or by displacement using scrap iron. Electrolysis is also used to purify impure copper, e.g. the metal obtained from smelting.

- Scientists are developing ways to extract copper that use low-grade copper ores. Bacteria are used in bioleaching and plants in phytomining.

- Copper can be extracted from **copper-rich ores** by **smelting**. This means heating the ore strongly in a furnace.

- Smelting produces impure copper, which can be purified by electrolysis.

- Look at Figure 1.
  – At the negative copper electrode (cathode) we get reduction:
  $$Cu^{2+}(aq) + 2e^- \rightarrow Cu(s)$$
  – At the positive copper electrode (anode) we get oxidation:
  $$Cu(s) \rightarrow Cu^{2+}(aq) + 2e^-$$

- The copper can also be extracted from copper sulfate solution in industry by adding scrap iron. Iron is more reactive than copper, so it can displace copper from its solutions:
  $$\text{iron} + \text{copper(II) sulfate} \rightarrow \text{iron(II) sulfate} + \text{copper}$$

- Smelting and purifying copper ore require huge amounts of heating and electricity.

- Copper-rich ores are a limited resource. Scientists are developing new ways of extracting copper from low-grade ores. These methods can have less environmental impact than smelting.

- **Phytomining** uses plants to absorb copper compounds from the ground. The plants are burned and produce ash from which copper can be extracted.

- **Bioleaching** uses bacteria to produce solutions containing copper compounds.

> ⫸ **1** Why are new ways of extracting copper being researched?
>
> ⫸ **2** What three ways can be used to produce copper metal from its compounds?

Figure 2 Pure copper plates produced by electrolysis

Impure copper anode gets smaller

Very pure copper at the cathode

Sludge containing precious metals

Solution containing copper ions

Figure 1 In industry copper electrodes are used to obtain very pure copper metal. Impure copper from smelting is made the positive electrode and pure copper is made the negative electrode. The negative electrode gradually gets bigger. Many of these cells operate at the same time and the pure copper is removed about every two weeks.

∞ **links**

Revise more about the half equations at electrodes in electrolysis in 14.2 'Changes at the electrodes'.

Key words: copper-rich ore, smelting, phytomining, bioleaching

C7.5 Recycling metals

Key points

- There are social, economic and environmental issues associated with exploiting metal ores.
- Recycling metals saves energy and our limited, non-renewable metal ores (and fossil fuels). The pollution caused by the mining and extraction of metals is also reduced.

Study tip

To gain the highest grade, you should be able to write a clear evaluation of information you are given about exploiting metal ores, identifying benefits and drawbacks and giving a conclusion.

⬭ links

Revise more about the production of aluminium in 14.3 'The extraction of aluminium'.

Figure 2 Recycling cans saves energy, as well as our limited supplies of metal ores, and reduces pollution

⬭ links

Revise more on the extraction of iron and production of steel in 7.9 'Iron and steels', and about the pollution caused by fossil fuels in 9.3 'Burning fuels'.

- Mining for metal ores involves digging up and processing large amounts of rock. This can produce large amounts of waste material and effect large areas of the environment.
- Recycling metals requires less energy than is needed to extract a metal.
- Recycling saves resources because less ore needs to be mined. Also, less fossil fuel is needed to provide the energy for the recycling process.
- As a result of these two factors, less pollution is produced by recycling metals compared with extracting metals from their ores.
- For example, comparing recycled aluminium with aluminium extracted from its ore, there is a 95% energy saving. The extraction of aluminium involves melting aluminium oxide that has been separated from its ore, and its electrolysis. The process requires huge amounts of electrical energy.

Figure 1 Steel girders are used in many buildings

▐▐▐➡ **1** *Why should we recycle aluminium cans?*

- Iron and steel, for example from the bodywork and engines of scrap cars, are also recycled. 'Tin cans' are another source of scrap iron. These are usually steel cans with a very thin coating of tin to prevent rusting. The cans are easy to separate from other domestic rubbish as they are magnetic.
- Using recycled steel saves about 50% of the energy used to extract iron from its ore and turn it into steel.
- Copper is another metal that gets recycled. However, this is difficult because copper is often alloyed with other metals.

▐▐▐➡ **2** *The copper used to make electrical wiring needs to have a high purity. Why is it often difficult to obtain pure copper by recycling scrap copper?*

C7.6 # Bonding in metals

Key points

- The atoms in metals are closely packed together and arranged in regular layers.
- The electrons in the highest energy level are delocalised. The strong electrostatic forces between these electrons and the positively charged metal ions hold the metal together.

- The atoms in a metallic element are all the same size. They form giant structures in which layers of atoms are arranged in regular patterns.
- You can make models of metal structures by stacking lots of small same-sized spheres, like marbles or polystyrene balls, together.

▷ **1** *How are the atoms arranged in a metal?*

- When metal atoms pack together, the electrons in the highest energy level (the outer electrons) delocalise and can move freely between atoms.
- This produces a lattice of positive ions in a 'sea' of moving electrons.
- The **delocalised electrons** strongly attract the positive ions and hold the giant structure together.

Figure 1 The close-packed arrangement of copper atoms in copper metal

Metal's outer electron

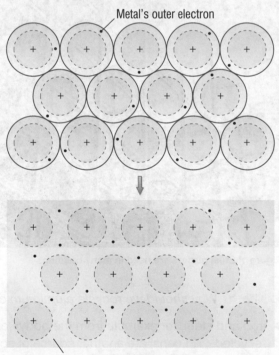

The 'sea' of delocalised electrons

Figure 2 A metal consists of positively charged metal ions surrounded by a 'sea' of delocalised electrons. This diagram shows us a model of metallic bonding.

links

Revise more about explaining the properties of metals in 7.7 'Giant metallic structures'.

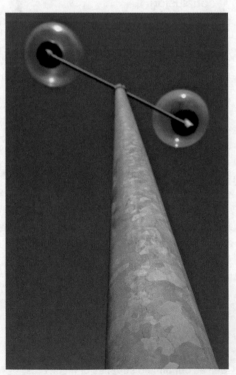

Figure 3 Metal crystals, such as the zinc ones shown on this galvanised lamp post, give us evidence that metals are made up of atoms arranged in regular patterns

Key word: delocalised electron

▷ **2** *What forces hold metal atoms in place in their giant structures?*

Giant metallic structures

Key points

- We can bend and shape metals because the layers of atoms (or positively charged ions) in a giant metallic structure can slide over each other.

- Delocalised electrons in metals enable electricity and heat to pass through a metal easily.

- Alloys are harder than pure metals because the regular layers in a pure metal are distorted by differently-sized atoms in an alloy.

- If a shape memory alloy is deformed, it can return to its original shape on heating.

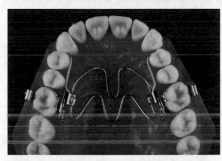

Figure 2 This dental brace pulls the teeth into the right position as it warms up. It is made of a shape memory alloy called nitinol. It is an alloy of nickel and titanium.

⬭ links

Revise more about the delocalised electrons in metals in 7.6 'Bonding in metals'.

- Metal atoms are arranged in layers. When a force is applied the layers of atoms can slide over each other. They can move into a new position without breaking apart, so the metal bends or stretches into a new shape. Metals are described as ductile and malleable, which makes them useful for making wires, rods and sheet materials.

▶ **1** *Why can metals be made into wires?*

- **Alloys** are mixtures of metals or metals mixed with other elements. The different-sized atoms in the mixture distort the regular pattern of atoms in the layers of the metal structure and make it more difficult for them to slide over each other. This makes alloys harder than pure metals.

- **Shape memory alloys** can be bent or deformed into a different shape. When they are heated they return to their original shape. They can be used in many ways, for example as dental braces.

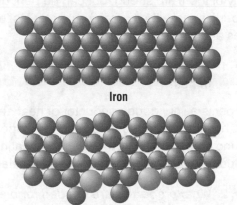

Iron

Alloy of iron

Figure 1 The atoms in pure iron are arranged in layers that can easily slide over each other. In alloys the layers cannot slide so easily because atoms of other elements change the regular structure.

▶ **2** *Give two reasons why alloys can be more useful than pure metals.*

- Metal structures have delocalised electrons. Metals are good conductors of heat and electricity because the delocalised electrons move throughout the **giant metallic lattice** and so can transfer energy quickly.

▶ **3** *Why are metals good conductors of electricity?*

Key words: alloy, shape memory alloy, giant metallic lattice

C7.8 Useful metals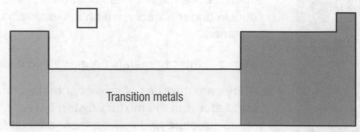

Key points

- The transition metals are found in the central block of the periodic table.

- Transition metals have properties that make them useful for building and making things.

- Most of the metals we use are alloys. For example copper, gold and aluminium are all alloyed with other metals to make them harder.

⚬⚬ links

Revise more about the properties of transition metals in 5.3 'The transition elements'.

- Elements from the central block of the periodic table are known as the **transition metals**.

Figure 1 The position of the transition metals in the periodic table

- They are all metals and have similar properties.
- They are good conductors of heat and electricity.
- Many of them are strong, but can be bent or hammered into shape. These properties make them useful as materials for buildings, vehicles, cargo containers, pipes and wires.

> **1** *What properties make transition metals useful materials for making things?*

- Copper is a very good conductor of heat and does not react with water. It can be bent but it is hard enough to keep its shape. These properties make it useful for making pipes and tanks in water and heating systems. It is a very good conductor of electricity as well and so it is used for electrical wiring.

> **2** *What properties are needed for electrical wiring?*

- Most of the metals we use are not pure elements.
- Pure iron, copper, gold and aluminium are soft and easily bent. They are often mixed with other elements to make alloys that are harder so that they keep their shape.
- Iron is made into steels (see 7.9).
- Gold used for jewellery is usually an alloy.
- Most of the aluminium used for buildings and aircraft is alloyed.
- Copper alloys include bronze and brass.

> **3** *Why is the gold used for wedding rings mixed with other metals?*

Study tip

When asked for the properties of alloys, many students include cost or cheapness but cost is not a property of a substance.

Key word: transition metal

Figure 2 Alloys are used to make some musical instruments

Iron and steels

Key points

- We extract iron from iron ore by reducing it using carbon in a blast furnace. The main reducing agent in the furnace is carbon monoxide gas.
- Pure iron is too soft for it to be very useful.
- Carefully controlled quantities of carbon and other elements are added to iron to make alloys of steel with different properties.
- Important examples of steels are:
  - low-carbon steels which are easily shaped
  - high-carbon steels which are very hard
  - stainless steels which are resistant to corrosion.

- Many of the ores used to produce iron contain iron(III) oxide. Iron(III) oxide is reduced at high temperatures in a **blast furnace** using carbon.
- The raw materials fed into the furnace are:
  - iron ore (called haematite)
  - coke (a cheap form of carbon made from coal)
  - limestone (used to remove impurities by reacting with them to form slag).
- The main reactions in the blast furnace are:

$$\text{carbon} + \text{oxygen} \rightarrow \text{carbon dioxide}$$
$$C(s) + O_2(g) \rightarrow CO_2(g)$$

The CO_2 made reacts with hot coke to make the main reducing agent, CO:

$$\text{carbon dioxide} + \text{carbon} \rightarrow \text{carbon monoxide}$$
$$CO_2(g) + C(s) \rightarrow 2CO(g)$$

Then carbon monoxide reduces the iron(III) oxide:

$$\text{iron(III) oxide} + \text{carbon monoxide} \rightarrow \text{iron} + \text{carbon dioxide}$$
$$Fe_2O_3(s) + 3CO(g) \rightarrow 2Fe(l) + 3CO_2(g)$$

The molten iron is tapped off from the bottom of the furnace.

- The iron produced contains about 96% iron. The impurities make it hard and brittle and so it has only a few uses as **cast iron**. Removing all of the carbon and other impurities makes pure iron, but this is too soft for many uses.

▶ **1** *Why does iron from the blast furnace have only a few uses?*

- Most iron is used to make **steels**. Steels are **alloys** of iron because they are mixtures of iron with carbon and other elements. Alloys can be made so that they have properties for specific uses.

Figure 1 Steels have many uses in modern buildings

- The amounts of carbon and other elements are carefully adjusted when making steels. Low-carbon steels are easily shaped and high-carbon steels are hard.
- Some steels, such as **stainless steels**, contain larger quantities of other metals, such as chromium and nickel. They resist corrosion.

Key words: blast furnace, cast iron, steel, alloy, stainless steel

▶ **2** *Why are steels more useful than pure iron?*

1 What is the name for rock that is mined and from which metal can be extracted economically?

2 Why can gold be found in the Earth as the element itself?

3 What are the typical properties of 'transition metals'?

4 Explain why most of the metals we use are not pure elements.

5 What type of chemical reaction is used to get iron from iron(III) oxide? Write a word equation for the reaction between iron(III) oxide and carbon.

6 Name three types of steel and give an important property for each one.

7 Explain why all steels are alloys.

8 Suggest three reasons why we should recycle iron and steel.

9 Balance these equations:

$$CO_2 + C \rightarrow CO$$
$$Fe_2O_3 + C \rightarrow Fe + CO_2$$
$$Fe_2O_3 + CO \rightarrow Fe + CO_2$$

10 Name two methods, other than smelting, of extracting copper from low-grade ores. Explain how one of these methods can be used to make copper.

11 Explain the bonding in metals and how this enables them to be good conductors of electricity.

Chapter checklist ✓ ✓ ✓

Tick when you have:				The reactivity series	▢	▢	▢
reviewed it after your lesson	✓	▢	▢	Displacement reactions	▢	▢	▢
revised once – some questions right	✓	✓	▢	Extracting metals	▢	▢	▢
revised twice – all questions right	✓	✓	✓	Extracting copper	▢	▢	▢
Move on to another topic when you have all three ticks				Recycling metals	▢	▢	▢
				Bonding in metals	▢	▢	▢
				Giant metallic structures	▢	▢	▢
				Useful metals	▢	▢	▢
				Iron and steels	▢	▢	▢

How fast?

Key points

- We can find the rate of a chemical reaction by measuring the amount of reactants used up over time or by measuring the amount of products made over time.

- The gradient or slope of the line on a graph of amount of reactant or product against time tells us the rate of reaction at that time. The steeper the gradient, the faster the reaction.

▶ **1** *What two types of measurement must be made to find the average rate of a reaction?*

▶ **2** *How can we use a graph of amount of product against time to tell us the rate of the reaction at a given time?*

▶ **3** *How would the line on the Figure 2 graph differ if you plot 'Loss in mass' on the vertical axis?*

Study tip

The faster the rate, the shorter the time it takes for the reaction to finish. So rate is **inversely proportional** to time.

Key word: gradient

- The rate of a reaction measures the speed of a reaction or how fast it is. The rate can be found by measuring how much of a reactant is used, or how much of a product is formed, and the time taken.

- Alternatively the rate can be found by measuring the time taken for a certain amount of reactant to be used or product to be formed. These methods give the average rate for the time measured.

$$\text{Rate of reaction} = \frac{\text{amount of reactant used}}{\text{time}} \text{ or } \frac{\text{amount of product formed}}{\text{time}}$$

- An average rate can also be found by measuring the time it takes for a certain amount of solid to appear in a solution. If a gas is given off in the reaction, its average rate can be found by measuring the time taken to collect a certain volume of gas.

- The rate of a reaction at any given time can be found from the **gradient**, or slope, of the line on a graph of amount of reactant or product against time. The steeper the gradient, the faster the reaction is at that time.

- A graph can be produced by measuring the mass of gas released or the volume of gas produced at intervals of time. Other possible ways include measuring changes in the colour, concentration, or pH of a reaction mixture over time.

Practical

Measuring rates of reaction

If a reaction gives off a gas, we can monitor the rate of reaction by measuring how quickly the **mass** of a reaction mixture decreases.

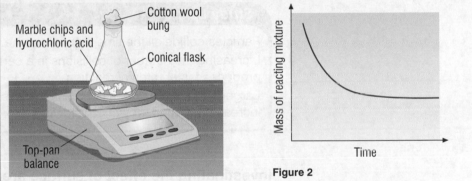

Figure 1

Figure 2

Alternatively, if a reaction produces a gas, we collect the gas and measure the volume given off at time intervals.

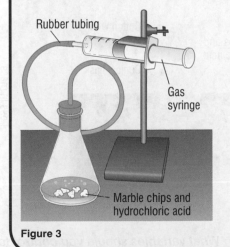

Figure 3

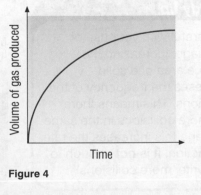

Figure 4

Student Book
pages 104–105

C8.2 Collision theory and surface area

- The **collision theory** states that reactions can only happen if particles collide.
- However, just colliding is not enough. The particles must collide with enough energy to change into new substances. The minimum energy they need to react is called the **activation energy**.

▶ **1** *What do we call the minimum energy needed for particles to react?*

- Factors that increase the frequency of collisions, or the energy of the particles, will increase the rate of the reaction.
  Increasing the:
  - temperature
  - concentration of solutions
  - pressure of gases
  - surface area of solids, and
  - using a catalyst
  will increase the rate of a reaction.
- Breaking large pieces of a solid into smaller pieces exposes new surfaces and so increases the surface area. This means there are more collisions in the same time. So a powder reacts faster than large lumps of a substance. The finer the powder the faster the reaction.

▶ **2** *Why do powders react faster than large pieces of solid?*

Key points

- Particles must collide with a certain amount of energy before they can react.
- The minimum amount of energy that particles must have in order to react is called the activation energy.
- The rate of a chemical reaction increases if the surface area of any solid reactants is increased. This increases the frequency of collisions between reacting particles.

∞ links

Revise more about activation energy in 12.6 'Energy level diagrams'.

Study tip

Particles collide all the time, but only some collisions lead to reactions.
Increasing the number of collisions in a certain time and the energy of collisions produces faster rates of reaction.
Larger surface area does not result in collisions with more energy but does increase the frequency of collisions.

Investigating the effect of surface area

In this investigation, the mass lost against time for different sizes of marble (calcium carbonate) chips can be monitored. At least two different sizes of marble chips are needed in order to vary the surface area.

Study tip

Be careful with your use of language: increasing the surface area of a solid increases the frequency of the collisions. This means there are more collisions in the same time and this increases the rate of reaction. It is **not** enough to just write 'more collisions'.

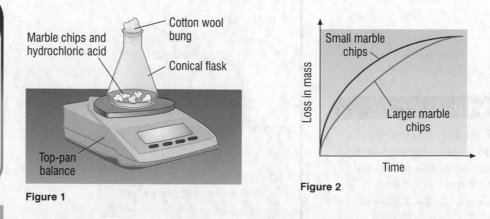

Figure 1

Figure 2

Key words: collision theory, activation energy

▶ **3** *What variables should you control to make this a fair test?*

C8.3 The effect of temperature

- Increasing the temperature increases the speed of the particles in a reaction mixture. This means they collide more often, which increases the rate of reaction. As well as colliding more frequently they collide with more energy, which also increases the rate of reaction.
- Therefore, a small change in temperature has a large effect on reaction rates. At ordinary temperatures a rise of 10°C will roughly double the rate of many reactions, so they go twice as fast.
- A decrease in temperature will slow reactions down, and a decrease of 10°C will double the time that many reactions take. This is why we refrigerate or freeze food so it stays fresh for longer.

1 *Why does a small change in temperature have a large effect on the rate of reaction?*

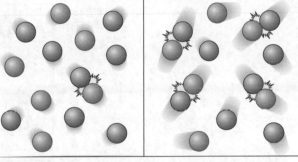

Figure 1 More frequent collisions, with more energy – both of these factors increase the rate of a chemical reaction caused by increasing the temperature

Practical

The effect of temperature on rate of reaction

When sodium thiosulfate solution and hydrochloric acid react, sulfur is formed. The sulfur is insoluble in water. This makes the solution go cloudy. The length of time it takes for the solution to go cloudy at different temperatures can be measured.

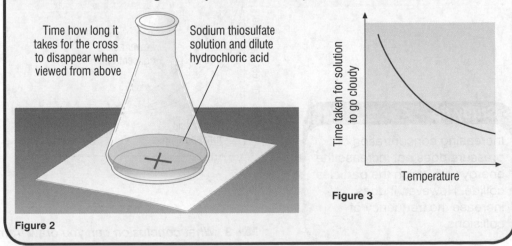

Figure 2

Figure 3

2 *Why is it difficult to get accurate timings by eye in this investigation?*

3 *How can you improve the precision of the data you collect?*

C8.4

The effect of concentration or pressure

Key points

- Increasing the concentration of reactants in solutions increases the frequency of collisions between particles, and so increases the rate of reaction.
- Increasing the pressure of reacting gases also increases the frequency of collisions and so increases the rate of reaction.

- The particles in a solution are moving around randomly. If the concentration of a solution is increased there are more particles dissolved in the same volume. This means the dissolved particles are closer together and so they collide more often.
- Increasing the concentration of a reactant therefore increases the rate of a reaction because the particles collide more frequently.

▶ **1** *Why do reactions in solutions go faster at higher concentrations?*

- In a similar way, increasing the pressure of a gas puts more molecules into the same volume, and so they collide more frequently. This increases the rate of reactions that have gases as reactants.

▶ **2** *Why does increasing the pressure increase the rate of a reaction of two gases?*

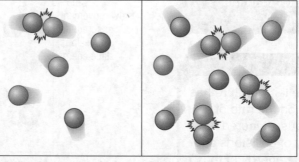

Low concentration/low pressure   High concentration/high pressure

Figure 1 Increasing concentration and pressure mean that particles are closer together. This increases the frequency of collisions between particles, so the reaction rate increases.

- An investigation monitored the mass of the reaction mixture as three different concentrations of hydrochloric acid reacted with calcium carbonate. If we plot the results of the investigation on a graph, they look like the graph below:

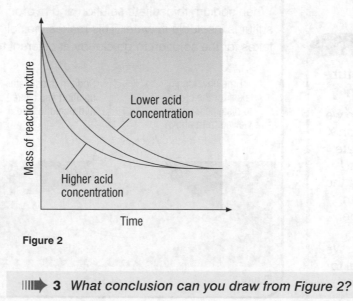

Figure 2

Study tip

Increasing concentration or pressure does not increase the energy with which the particles collide. However, it does increase the frequency of collisions.

▶ **3** *What conclusion can you draw from Figure 2?*

C8.5 The effect of catalysts

- A catalyst speeds up the rate of a chemical reaction but is not used up itself during the reaction. It remains chemically unchanged.
- Different catalysts are needed for different reactions.
- Catalysts are used whenever possible in industry to increase rates of reaction and reduce energy costs.

- **Catalysts** change the rates of chemical reactions. Most catalysts are used to speed up reactions. Catalysts that speed up reactions lower the activation energy of the reaction so that more of the collisions result in a reaction.
- Although the catalyst changes the rate of the reaction it is not used up. The catalyst is left at the end of the reaction and so it can be used over and over again.

⮕ **1** *Why can catalysts be used over and over again?*

- Catalysts that are solids are used in forms that have large surface areas to make them as effective as possible.
- Catalysts often work with only one type of reaction and so different reactions need different catalysts.
- Some catalysts are expensive but they can be economical because they do not need replacing very often. They are used in many industrial processes because they can reduce the energy and the time needed for reactions. This helps to reduce costs and reduce impacts on the environment. If fossil fuels are burned to provide energy for industrial reactions, using catalysts will help to conserve resources and reduce pollution.
- Many of the catalysts used in industry involve transition metals and their compounds. Some of these metals and their compounds are toxic and may cause harm if they get into the environment.

⮕ **2 a** *What are the benefits of using catalysts in industrial processes?*
   b *Give one disadvantage of transition metal catalysts.*

Practical

Investigating catalysis

The effect of different catalysts on the rate of a reaction can be investigated using the decomposition of hydrogen peroxide:

$$2H_2O_2(aq) \rightarrow 2H_2O(l) + O_2(g)$$

The reaction produces oxygen gas. The gas can be collected in a gas syringe as shown above.

We can investigate the effect of many different substances on the rate of this reaction. Examples include manganese(IV) oxide, MnO_2, and potassium iodide, KI.

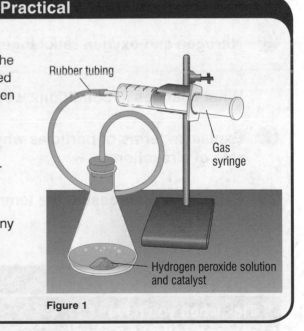

Rubber tubing

Gas syringe

Hydrogen peroxide solution and catalyst

Figure 1

⮕ **3** *In this investigation, a group decided to measure the time taken to collect 20 cm³ of gas for each different potential catalyst. What type of graph should they use to display their results?*

Catalysts change only the rate of reactions. They do not change the products.

Key word: catalyst

1   Pieces of zinc react with dilute hydrochloric acid:

$$Zn(s) + 2HCl(aq) \rightarrow ZnCl_2(aq) + H_2(g)$$

In what ways could you increase the rate of the reaction between zinc and hydrochloric acid?

2   Give two ways in which you could monitor the rate of reaction of magnesium and dilute hydrochloric acid by experiment.

3   How can you find the rate of a reaction from a graph of mass of product against time?

4   What is meant by the 'activation energy' of a reaction?

5   Iron reacts with dilute sulfuric acid. Given the same mass of iron under the same conditions, which form of iron will react fastest when acid is added and which will react slowest:

iron wool   iron filings   iron nails   a block of iron

6   What is a catalyst?

7   State two pieces of apparatus that could be used to measure the volume of a gas liberated as a reaction takes place.

8   Nitrogen and oxygen react together to produce nitrogen oxide:

$$N_2(g) + O_2(g) \rightarrow 2NO(g)$$

What changes in conditions would increase the rate of this reaction?

9   Explain in terms of particles why increasing the concentration of a reactant increases the rate of a reaction.

10 Explain why increasing the temperature increases the rate of a reaction.

Chapter checklist		✓ ✓ ✓
Tick when you have:	How fast?	☐ ☐ ☐
reviewed it after your lesson ☑ ☐ ☐	Collision theory and surface area	☐ ☐ ☐
revised once – some questions right ☑ ☑ ☐	The effect of temperature	☐ ☐ ☐
revised twice – all questions right ☑ ☑ ☑	The effect of concentration or pressure	☐ ☐ ☐
Move on to another topic when you have all three ticks	The effect of catalysts	☐ ☐ ☐

1 Sodium thiosulfate solution reacts with hydrochloric acid as shown in this equation.

$$Na_2S_2O_3(aq) + 2HCl(aq) \rightarrow 2NaCl(aq) + S(s) + SO_2(g) + H_2O(l)$$

Solutions of the reactants are mixed in a conical flask to investigate the rate of reaction.

The rate of this reaction can be found by timing how long it takes for a mark on a piece of paper placed beneath the conical flask to disappear from view.

a Explain why the cross disappears from view. Include the name of the type of reaction being investigated. *(3 marks)*

b A student wants to compare the results she gets for different concentrations of sodium thiosulfate solution. Her teacher only provides one concentration of sodium thiosulfate solution which is $120\,g/dm^3$. Describe how the student can make different known concentrations of sodium thiosulfate solution for use in her experiments. *(2 marks)*

c Name two variables that the student should control to ensure a fair test. *(2 marks)*

The graph shows results from her experiments.

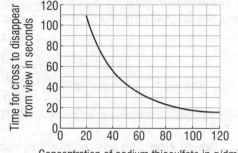

d i How does the time taken for the mark to disappear from view change as the concentration of sodium thiosulfate increases? *(1 mark)*

ii What effect does concentration have on the rate of this reaction? *(2 marks)*

iii Explain your answer to **ii** using ideas about particles in your answer. *(3 marks)*

e *In this question you will be assessed on using good English, organising information clearly and using specialist terms where appropriate.*

Write a plan that you could use to investigate the effect of temperature on the rate of reaction between sodium thiosulfate solution and dilute hydrochloric acid.

You should include how to carry out the fair test, any apparatus you will need and appropriate safety precautions. *(6 marks)*

2 Zinc is obtained from its ore zinc blende, containing the compound zinc sulfide (ZnS).

a Why is zinc blende an example of an 'ore'? *(1 mark)*

b Why is zinc sulfide called a 'compound'? *(1 mark)*

The extraction of zinc is carried out with a blast furnace. Firstly, the zinc sulfide is converted to zinc oxide (ZnO) by roasting in air where it reacts with oxygen (O_2). The gas sulfur dioxide (SO_2) is given off.

c i Write a word equation for the roasting of zinc sulfide in air. *(1 mark)*

ii Write a balanced symbol equation, including state symbols, for the reaction. *(3 marks)*

Then the zinc oxide is heated with carbon (in the form of coke) in the blast furnace.

As with iron, the main reducing agent in the blast furnace is carbon monoxide:

$$2C(s) + O_2(g) \rightarrow 2CO(g)$$

This carbon monoxide gas converts the zinc oxide to zinc.

d i Write a word equation for the conversion of zinc oxide to zinc. *(1 mark)*

ii Explain in detail what happens to the zinc ions (Zn^{2+}) in zinc oxide when the zinc metal is extracted, in terms of the electron transfer involved. *(3 marks)*

C9.1 Hydrocarbons

Key points

- Crude oil is a mixture of many different compounds.
- Most of the compounds in crude oil are hydrocarbons – they contain only hydrogen and carbon.
- Alkanes are saturated hydrocarbons. They contain as many hydrogen atoms as possible in their molecules.
- The general formula of an alkane is: $C_nH_{(2n+2)}$

- Crude oil contains many different compounds that boil at different temperatures. These burn under different conditions and so crude oil needs to be separated to make useful fuels.
- We can separate a **mixture** of liquids by **distillation**. Simple distillation of crude oil can produce liquids that boil within different temperature ranges. These liquids are called **fractions**.

▐▶ **1** *What are fractions?*

- Most of the compounds in crude oil are **hydrocarbons**. This means that their molecules contain only hydrogen and carbon. Many of these hydrocarbons are **alkanes**, with the general formula $C_nH_{(2n+2)}$. Alkanes contain as many hydrogen atoms as possible in each molecule and so we call them **saturated hydrocarbons**.
- Look at the formulae of the first five alkane molecules below:

$$CH_4 \text{ (methane)}$$
$$C_2H_6 \text{ (ethane)}$$
$$C_3H_8 \text{ (propane)}$$
$$C_4H_{10} \text{ (butane)}$$
$$C_5H_{12} \text{ (pentane)}$$

▐▶ **2** *How can you tell that the substance with the formula C_9H_{20} is an alkane?*

- We can represent molecules in different ways. A molecular formula shows the number of each type of atom in each molecule, e.g. C_2H_6 represents a molecule of ethane. We can also represent molecules by a displayed formula that shows how the atoms are bonded together.

links

To revise covalent bonding, look back at 3.4 'Covalent bonding'.

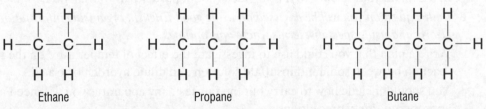

Ethane   Propane   Butane

Figure 1 We can represent alkanes like this, showing all of the atoms and the covalent bonds in each molecule

Study tip

Remember that the boiling point of a substance is the temperature at which its liquid boils when it is heated. When its gas is cooled it condenses at the same temperature.

▐▶ **3** *What is the molecular formula of butane?*

Key words: mixture, distillation, fraction, hydrocarbon, alkane, saturated hydrocarbon

C9.2 # Fractional distillation

Key points

- Crude oil is separated into fractions using fractional distillation.
- The properties of each fraction depend on the size of the hydrocarbon molecules in it.
- Lighter fractions make better fuels as they ignite more easily and burn well, with cleaner (less smoky) flames.

- Crude oil is separated into fractions at refineries using **fractional distillation**. This can be done because the boiling point of a hydrocarbon depends on the size of its molecules. The larger the molecules are, the higher the boiling point of the hydrocarbon.

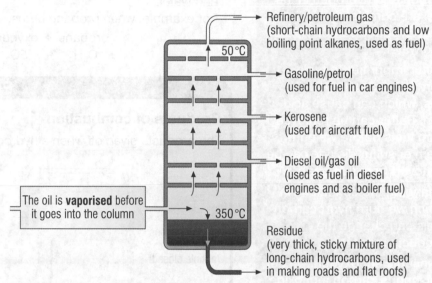

Figure 1 We use fractional distillation to separate crude oil into fractions. Each fraction contains compounds with similar boiling points.

- The crude oil is vaporised and fed into a fractionating column. This is a tall tower that is hot at the bottom and gets cooler going up the column.

> **Study tip**
>
> Simple distillation is done in steps by heating the mixture to different temperatures. Fractional distillation is done continuously by vaporising the mixture and condensing the fractions at different temperatures.

- Inside the column there are many trays with holes to allow gases through. The vapours move up the column getting cooler as they go up. The hydrocarbons condense to liquids when they reach the level that is at their boiling point. Different liquids collect on the trays at different levels and there are outlets to collect the fractions.

- Hydrocarbons with the smallest molecules have the lowest boiling points and so are collected at the top of the column. The fractions collected at the bottom of the column contain hydrocarbons with the highest boiling points.

Figure 2 An oil refinery at night

▐▐▐➡ **1** *Why are different hydrocarbons collected at different levels of a fractional distillation column?*

- Fractions with low boiling ranges have low **viscosity** so they are runny liquids. They are very **flammable** so they ignite easily. They also burn with clean flames, producing little smoke. This makes them very useful as fuels.

Key words: fractional distillation, viscosity, flammable

▐▐▐➡ **2** *What properties would you expect for a fraction that is collected one-third of the way up a fractionating column?*

Student Book
pages 118–119

C9.3 Burning fuels

- Burning any fuel that contains carbon produces carbon dioxide, which is a greenhouse gas. Many scientists believe that increased atmospheric carbon dioxide is the cause of **global warming**.
- When pure hydrocarbons burn completely they are **oxidised** to carbon dioxide and water.
  For example, when propane burns:

$$\text{propane} + \text{oxygen} \rightarrow \text{carbon dioxide} + \text{water}$$
$$C_3H_8 + 5O_2 \rightarrow 3CO_2 + 4H_2O$$

Practical

Products of combustion

The products given off when a hydrocarbon burns can be tested as shown below.

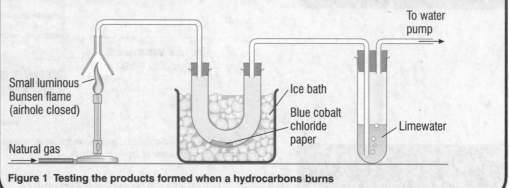

Figure 1 Testing the products formed when a hydrocarbons burns

▐▶ **1 a** *What happens to the limewater? Which gas is given off?*
   b *What happens in the U-tube? Which substance is present?*

▐▶ **2** *Write a word equation for the complete combustion of ethane.*

- However, the fuels we use are not always burned completely and may also contain other substances. In a limited supply of air **incomplete combustion** may produce **carbon monoxide** (CO – a toxic gas). For example, the incomplete combustion of methane:

$$2CH_4 + 3O_2 \rightarrow 2CO + 4H_2O$$

- Carbon may also be produced by incomplete combustion and some of the hydrocarbons may not burn. This produces solid particles that contain soot (carbon) and unburnt hydrocarbons called **particulates**. These particulates can cause lung damage, as well as **global dimming** as they prevent some sunlight reaching the Earth's surface.

▐▶ **3** *Name four possible products of the incomplete combustion of a hydrocarbon.*

- Most fossil fuels contain sulfur compounds. When the fuel burns, these sulfur compounds produce **sulfur dioxide** gas (SO_2). Sulfur dioxide causes acid rain.
- At the high temperatures produced when fuels burn, oxygen and nitrogen in the air may combine to form **nitrogen oxides**. Nitrogen oxides also cause acid rain, as well as breathing problems.

▐▶ **4** *What environmental problem is caused by sulfur dioxide and nitrogen oxides?*

Key points

- When we burn hydrocarbon fuels in plenty of air the carbon and hydrogen in the fuel are completely oxidised. They produce carbon dioxide and water.
- Sulfur impurities in fuels burn to form sulfur dioxide gas, which can cause acid rain. Sulfur can be removed from fuels before we burn them or sulfur dioxide can be removed from flue gas.
- Changing the conditions in which we burn hydrocarbon fuels can change the products made.
- In insufficient oxygen, we get poisonous carbon monoxide gas formed. We can also get particulates of carbon (soot) and unburnt hydrocarbons, especially if the fuel is diesel. They can cause global dimming.
- At the high temperatures in engines, nitrogen from the air reacts with oxygen to form oxides of nitrogen. These cause breathing problems and can also cause acid rain.

Study tip

You should be able to write balanced symbol equations for the complete and incomplete combustion of a hydrocarbon when given its formula.

Key words: global warming, oxidised, incomplete combustion, carbon monoxide, particulate, global dimming, sulfur dioxide, nitrogen oxides

C9.4 Alternative fuels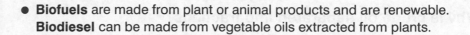

Key points

- Biofuels are a renewable source of energy that could be used to replace some fossil fuels.
- Biodiesel can be made from vegetable oils.
- There are advantages, and some disadvantages, in using biofuels.
- Ethanol is also a biofuel as it can be made from the sugar in plants.
- Hydrogen is a potential fuel for the future.

- **Biofuels** are made from plant or animal products and are renewable. **Biodiesel** can be made from vegetable oils extracted from plants.

Figure 1 This bus runs on biodiesel

- There are advantages to using biodiesel. For example, it makes little contribution to carbon dioxide levels. This is because the carbon dioxide given off when it burns was taken from the atmosphere by plants as they grew.
- There are also disadvantages, for example the plants that are grown for biodiesel use large areas of farmland.

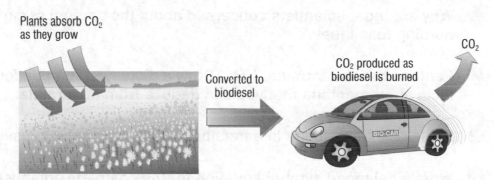

Figure 2 Cars run on biodiesel produce very little CO$_2$ overall, as CO$_2$ is absorbed by plants as the fuel is made

- Ethanol made from sugar cane or sugar beet is a biofuel. It is a liquid and so can be stored and distributed like other liquid fuels. It can be mixed with petrol.

||||⟹ **1** *Name two biofuels.*

- Using hydrogen as a fuel has the advantage that it produces only water when it is burned ($2H_2(g) + O_2(g) \rightarrow 2H_2O(g)$).
- However, it is a gas so it takes up a large volume. That makes it difficult to store in the quantities needed for combustion in engines.
- It can be produced from water by electrolysis but this requires large amounts of energy.

||||⟹ **2** *Give one advantage and one disadvantage of hydrogen as a fuel.*

Key words: biofuel, biodiesel

Figure 3 Ethanol can be made by fermenting the glucose from sugar cane

∞ links

To revise more about ethanol, see 11.2 'Properties and uses of alcohols'.

1. Why is crude oil separated into fractions?

2. Name the products when ethane, C_2H_6, burns completely i.e. undergoes complete combustion.

3. Give three reasons why fractions with lower boiling points are more useful as fuels.

4. Name two fuels that can be made from renewable sources.

5. Some exhaust fumes contain particulates. What are particulates and how are they produced?

6. a Explain why burning some fuels produces sulfur dioxide.

   b What two methods are used to reduce the amount of sulfur dioxide produced by burning fuels?

7. Propane, C_3H_8, is used as a fuel for cookers. Explain why propane should always be burned in a plentiful supply of air.

8. Why are most scientists concerned about the amount of carbon dioxide produced by burning fossil fuels?

9. Pentane has the formula C_5H_{12}. Draw a displayed formula for pentane and write down four facts about pentane that you can deduce from its formula.

10. Explain what happens in a fractional distillation column used to separate crude oil.

11. Write a balanced symbol equation for the complete combustion of ethanol, C_2H_6O.

12. Write a balanced symbol equation for the reaction of hydrogen with oxygen. Explain why scientists are interested in using hydrogen as a fuel.

Chapter checklist ✓ ✓ ✓

Tick when you have:

reviewed it after your lesson	✓	☐	☐	Fuels from crude oil	☐ ☐ ☐
revised once – some questions right	✓	✓	☐	Fractional distillation	☐ ☐ ☐
revised twice – all questions right	✓	✓	✓	Burning fuels	☐ ☐ ☐
				Alternative fuels	☐ ☐ ☐

Move on to another topic when you have all three ticks

Student Book
pages 124–125

C10.1

Cracking hydrocarbons

Key points

- We can break down large hydrocarbon molecules into smaller molecules by passing the vapours over a hot catalyst or by mixing them with steam and heating them to a very high temperature.

- Cracking produces saturated hydrocarbons (alkanes) which are used as fuels and unsaturated hydrocarbons (called alkenes).

- Alkenes (and other unsaturated compounds containing carbon–carbon double bonds) react with yellow-orange bromine water, turning it colourless.

- Ethene can be used to make ethanol by reacting it with steam in the presence of a catalyst.

- Large hydrocarbon molecules can be broken down into smaller molecules by a process called **cracking**.

- Cracking can be done in two ways: by heating a mixture of hydrocarbon vapours and steam to a very high temperature, or by passing hydrocarbon vapours over a hot catalyst.

- During cracking thermal decomposition reactions produce a mixture of smaller molecules. Some of the smaller molecules are alkanes, which are saturated hydrocarbons with the general formula C_nH_{2n+2}. The alkanes with smaller molecules are more useful as fuels.

> **1** *Give one reason why an oil company might want to crack large hydrocarbons to make smaller alkanes.*

- Some of the other smaller molecules formed are hydrocarbons with the general formula C_nH_{2n}. These are called alkenes. **Alkenes** are **unsaturated hydrocarbons** because they contain fewer hydrogen atoms than alkanes with the same number of carbon atoms.

$$C_{10}H_{22} \xrightarrow{\text{800°C + catalyst}} C_5H_{12} + C_3H_6 + C_2H_4$$
$$\text{decane} \qquad\qquad \text{pentane} \quad \text{propene} \quad \text{ethene}$$

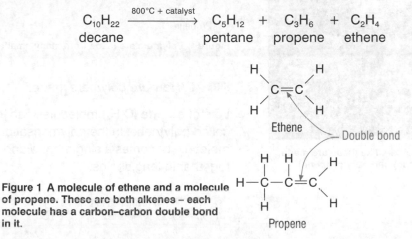

Figure 1 A molecule of ethene and a molecule of propene. These are both alkenes – each molecule has a carbon–carbon double bond in it.

- Alkenes have a **double bond** between two carbon atoms and this makes them more reactive than alkanes. Alkenes react with bromine water turning it from yellow-orange to colourless. This reaction is used as a test for unsaturated compounds.

> **2** *Give three ways in which alkenes are different from alkanes.*

- Ethanol for industrial use as a fuel or solvent can be made from ethene gas. Ethene can react with steam in the presence of a catalyst to make ethanol.

$$\text{ethene} + \text{steam} \xrightleftharpoons{\text{catalyst}} \text{ethanol}$$
$$C_2H_4 + H_2O \rightleftharpoons C_2H_5OH$$

Study tip

Different mixtures of alkanes and alkenes can be produced by cracking because different hydrocarbons can be used and the conditions for the reaction can be changed.

Figure 2 In an oil refinery huge crackers like this are used to break down large hydrocarbon molecules into smaller ones

Key words: cracking, alkene, unsaturated hydrocarbon, double bond

C10.2

Making polymers from alkenes

Key points

- Plastics are made of polymers.
- Polymers are large molecules made when many small molecules (monomers) join together.
- Alkenes can be used to make polymers such as poly(ethene) and poly(propene).

- Plastics are made of very large molecules called **polymers**. Polymers are made from many small molecules joined together. The small molecules used to make polymers are called **monomers**. The reaction to make a polymer is called **polymerisation**.

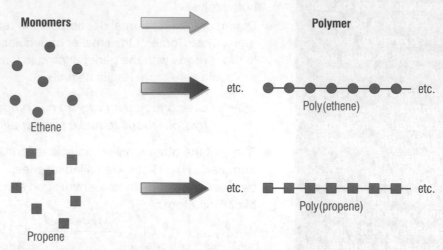

Figure 1 Polymers are made from many smaller molecules called monomers

Figure 2 Containers like these are made from poly(ethene) and poly(propene)

▐▐▶ **1** *How are polymers made?*

- Lots of **ethene** (C_2H_4) molecules can join together to form poly(ethene), commonly called polythene. In the polymerisation reaction the double bond in each ethene molecule becomes a single bond and thousands of ethene molecules join together in long chains.

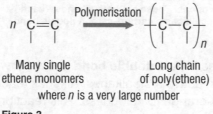

Figure 3

▐▐▶ **2** *How many monomers are there in a poly(ethene) molecule?*

- Other alkenes can polymerise in a similar way. For example, **propene** (C_3H_6), can form poly(propene).
- Many of the plastics we use as bags, bottles, containers and toys are made from alkenes.

▐▐▶ **3** *Why can we make polymers from alkenes but not from alkanes?*

Study tip

Learn to recognise monomers and polymers from diagrams. You should be able to draw the structure of the polymer made from a given monomer.

Key words: polymer, monomer, polymerisation, ethene, propene

Student Book
pages 132–133 **C10.3**

The properties of polymers

Key points

- The properties of polymers depend on the monomers used to make them.
- Changing reaction conditions can also change the properties of the polymer that is produced.
- Thermosoftening polymers will soften or melt easily when heated because their intermolecular forces are relatively weak.
- Thermosetting polymers will not soften because of their 'cross-linking' but will eventually char if heated very strongly.

- The properties of a polymer depend on the monomers used to make it, and the conditions we use to carry out the reaction. Poly(propene) is made from propene and softens at a higher temperature than poly(ethene), which is made from ethene. Low density (LD) poly(ethene) and high density (HD) poly(ethene) are made using different catalysts and different reaction conditions. HD poly(ethene) has a higher softening temperature and is stronger than LD poly(ethene).

1 *Why do LD and HD poly(ethene) have different properties?*

- Poly(ethene) is an example of a **thermosoftening polymer**. It is made up of individual polymer chains that are tangled together. When it is heated it becomes soft and hardens again when it cools. This means it can be heated to mould it into shape and it can be remoulded by heating it again.
- Other polymers called **thermosetting polymers** do not melt or soften when we heat them. These polymers set hard when they are first moulded because strong covalent bonds form cross-links between their polymer chains. The strong bonds hold the polymer chains in position.

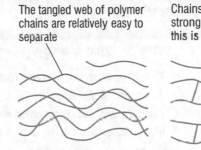

The tangled web of polymer chains are relatively easy to separate

Chains fixed together by strong covalent bonds – this is called **cross-linking**

Thermosoftening polymer   **Thermosetting** polymer

Figure 1 Extensive cross-linking by covalent bonds between polymer chains makes a thermosetting plastic that is heat-resistant and rigid

2 *What is the main difference in the structures of thermosoftening and thermosetting polymers?*

- In thermosoftening polymers the forces between the polymer chains are weak. When we heat the polymer, these weak intermolecular forces are broken and the polymer becomes soft. When the polymer cools down, the intermolecular forces bring the polymer molecules back together so the polymer hardens again.

3 *Why can thermosoftening polymers be remoulded?*

Figure 2 Electrical sockets and plugs are made using thermosetting plastics

Study tip

You should be able to recognise the type of polymer from a diagram of its structure or a description of its properties. Thermosetting polymers have covalent bonds linking the chains and do not soften when heated.

Key words: thermosoftening polymer, thermosetting polymer

Student Book
pages 130–131 **C10.4** # New and useful polymers

Key points

- New polymers are being developed all the time. They are designed to have properties that make them specially suited for certain uses.
- Smart polymers may have their properties changed by light, temperature or other changes in their surroundings.
- We are now recycling more plastics and finding new uses for them.

Study tip

You should know some of the ways that polymers are used but you do not have to remember the names of specific polymers.

- Materials scientists design new polymers to make materials with special properties for particular uses. Many of these materials are used for packaging, clothing and medical applications.
- New polymer materials for dental fillings have been developed to replace fillings that contain mercury. Light-sensitive polymers are used in sticking plasters to cover wounds so the plasters can be easily removed. Hydrogels are polymers that can trap water and have many uses including dressings for wounds.
- Shape-memory polymers change back to their original shape when temperature or other conditions are changed. An example of this type of **smart polymer** is a material used for stitching wounds that changes shape when heated to body temperature.

Figure 1 A shape-memory polymer uses the temperature of the body to make the thread tighten and close the wound

▐▐▐➡ **1** *What is a shape-memory polymer?*

- The fibres used to make fabrics can be coated with polymers to make them waterproof yet breathable.
- The plastic used to make many drinks bottles can be recycled to make polyester fibres for clothing as well as filling for pillows and duvets.

▐▐▐➡ **2** *Give two medical uses and two non-medical uses for polymers.*

Figure 2 Recycling bottles such as these can produce fibres for clothes or duvets

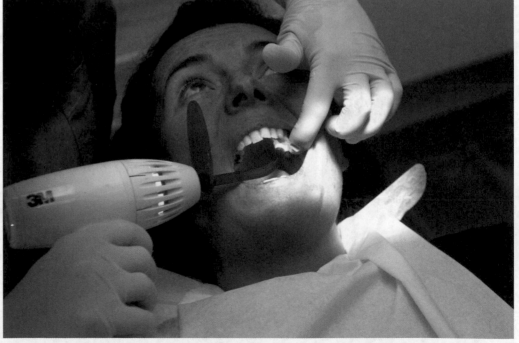

Figure 3 A dentist using UV light to set a filling made from a light-sensitive polymer

Key word: smart polymer

Plastic waste

Key points

- Non-biodegradable plastics cause unsightly rubbish, can harm wildlife and take up space in landfill sites.
- Biodegradable plastics are decomposed by the action of microorganisms in soil.
- Making plastics with starch granules in their structure helps the microorganisms break down a plastic.
- We can make biodegradable plastics from plant material such as cornstarch.

- Many polymers are not **biodegradable**. This means that plastic waste is not broken down when left in the environment. Unless disposed of properly, plastic rubbish gets everywhere. It is unsightly and can harm wildlife. Even when put into landfill sites it takes up valuable space.

Figure 1 Finding space to dump and bury our waste is becoming a big problem

- We are using more plastics that are biodegradable. Microorganisms can break down biodegradable plastics. These plastics break down when in contact with soil.

▶ **1** *How would using biodegradable plastics help with the problems of plastic litter?*

- Plastics made from non-biodegradable polymers can have cornstarch mixed into the plastic. Microorganisms break down the cornstarch so the plastic breaks down into very small pieces that can be mixed with soil or compost.
- Biodegradable plastics can be made from plant material. One example is a polymer made from cornstarch that is used as biodegradable food packaging.
- Some plastics can be recycled but there are many different types of plastic and sorting is difficult.

▶ **2** *Describe the two ways that cornstarch can be used to help with the disposal problems of plastic waste.*

Key word: biodegradable

Figure 2 The breakdown of a biodegradable polymer. PLA – poly(lactic acid) – can be designed to break down in a few months.

∞ links

To revise more on the issues of using biofuels, look back at 9.4 'Alternative fuels'.

1   Give two reasons why fractions from crude oil are cracked.

2   Describe two ways that are used in an oil refinery to crack hydrocarbons.

3   Sort these formulae into alkanes and alkenes:

$$C_3H_6, C_5H_{12}, C_4H_{10}, C_4H_8, C_6H_{14}$$

4   Poly(ethene) is a polymer. Explain what is meant by 'a polymer'.

5   Describe one use of a smart polymer.

6   Some plastics are biodegradable. What does 'biodegradable' mean?

7   Suggest three ways of reducing the problems of plastic rubbish.

8   Ethanol can be used as a fuel. It can be made by the fermentation of sugars from plant material or by hydrating ethene obtained by cracking products from crude oil. Give an advantage and a disadvantage of each method.

9   a   Write an equation using displayed formulae showing the bonds for the polymerisation of propene.

   b   Write a balanced equation showing the hydration of ethene.

10   Copy and complete this equation for the cracking of a hydrocarbon:

$$C_{12}H_{26} \rightarrow C_6H_{14} + C_4H_8 + ...$$

11   Why are thermosetting polymers often used to make handles for cooking pans?

12   Polymers made from different monomers have different properties. Explain why.

Chapter checklist	✓ ✓ ✓

Tick when you have:
reviewed it after your lesson — ✓ ☐ ☐
revised once – some questions right — ✓ ✓ ☐
revised twice – all questions right — ✓ ✓ ✓

Move on to another topic when you have all three ticks

Cracking hydrocarbons	☐	☐	☐
Making polymers from alkenes	☐	☐	☐
The properties of polymers	☐	☐	☐
New and useful polymers	☐	☐	☐
Plastic waste	☐	☐	☐

Student Book
pages 136–137 **C11.1**

Structures of alcohols, carboxylic acids and esters

Key points

- The homologous series of alcohols contain the —OH functional group.
- The homologous series of carboxylic acids contain the —COOH functional group.
- The homologous series of esters contains the —COO— functional group.

Study tip

If you draw displayed formulae, make sure you show all the bonds, including those in the functional group (as lines between atoms) and all the atoms (as their chemical symbols).

∞ links

To revise more about the homologous series of carboxylic acids and esters, see 11.3 'Carboxylic acids and esters'.

- Organic molecules form the basis of living things and all contain carbon atoms. Carbon atoms bond covalently to each other to form the 'backbone' of many series of organic molecules.
- Series of molecules that have a general formula are called **homologous series**. The alkanes and the alkenes are two homologous series made of only hydrogen and carbon atoms.

▸ **1** *Name the first three members of the alkanes.*

- Alcohols contain the **functional group** —O—H. If one hydrogen atom from each alkane molecule is replaced with an —O—H group, we get a homologous series of alcohols.
- The first three members of this series are methanol, ethanol and propanol.

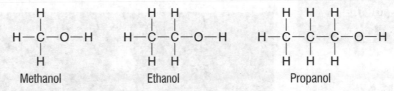

Methanol   Ethanol   Propanol

Figure 1 The displayed formulae of the first three members of the alcohol series

- A structural formula shows which atoms are bonded to each carbon atom and the functional group. The structural formula of ethanol is CH_3CH_2OH.

▸ **2** *Write the structural formula of propanol.*

- Carboxylic acids have the functional group —COOH.
- The first three members of the carboxylic acids are methanoic acid, ethanoic acid and propanoic acid. Their structural formulae are HCOOH, CH_3COOH and CH_3CH_2COOH.

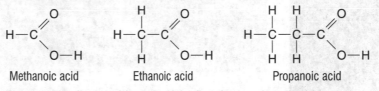

Methanoic acid   Ethanoic acid   Propanoic acid

Figure 2 The displayed formula of the first three carboxylic acids

▸ **3** *Draw the displayed formula of methanoic acid.*

- Esters have the functional group —COO—. If the H atom in the —COOH group of a carboxylic acid is replaced by a hydrocarbon group the compound is an ester.
- Ethyl ethanoate has the structural formula $CH_3COOCH_2CH_3$. (See Figure 3.)

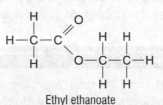

Ethyl ethanoate

Figure 3 The displayed formula of ethyl ethanoate

Key words: homologous series, functional group

71

Student Book
pages 138–139 **C11.2**

Properties and uses of alcohols

Student Book
pages 138–139

Key points

- Alcohols are used as solvents and fuels, and ethanol is the main alcohol in alcoholic drinks.
- Alcohols burn in air, forming carbon dioxide and water.
- Alcohols react with sodium to form a solution and give off hydrogen gas.
- Ethanol can be oxidised to ethanoic acid, either by chemical oxidising agents or by the action of microbes. Ethanoic acid is the main acid in vinegar.

⊂⊃ links

To revise how ethanol is manufactured from ethene see 10.1 'Cracking hydrocarbons'.

- Alcohols with smaller molecules, such as methanol, ethanol and propanol, mix well with water and produce neutral solutions.
- Many organic substances dissolve in alcohols and so this makes them useful solvents.
- Ethanol is the main alcohol in wine, beer and other alcoholic drinks. This ethanol is manufactured by fermentation, in which yeast (a fungus) is used to convert glucose (from plant material) into ethanol plus carbon dioxide.

▶ **1** *Why do many perfumes contain ethanol?*

- Alcohols burn in air. When burned completely they produce carbon dioxide and water. They are used as fuels, for example in spirit burners or in combustion engines and they can be mixed with petrol.

$$\text{ethanol} + \text{oxygen} \rightarrow \text{carbon dioxide} + \text{water}$$
$$C_2H_5OH + 3O_2 \rightarrow 2CO_2 + 3H_2O$$

Figure 1 Alcohols are flammable. They produce carbon dioxide and water in their combustion reactions.

- Sodium reacts with alcohols to produce hydrogen gas, but the reactions are less vigorous than when sodium reacts with water.
- Alcohols can be oxidised by chemical oxidising agents such as potassium dichromate to produce carboxylic acids. Some microbes in the air can also oxidise solutions of ethanol to produce ethanoic acid, which turns alcoholic drinks sour and is the main acid in vinegar.

▶ **2** *Ethanol and water are both colourless liquids. Suggest one chemical test you could do to tell them apart.*

Study tip

You should know the main reactions of alcohols and how to tell if a liquid is an alcohol, an alkane, an acid or water.

Figure 2 Alcohols are used as solvents in perfumes

Carboxylic acids and esters

Key points

- Solutions of carboxylic acids have a pH value less than 7. Carbonates gently fizz in their acidic solutions, releasing carbon dioxide gas.

- Aqueous solutions of weak acids, such as carboxylic acids, have a higher pH value than solutions of strong acids with the same concentration.

- Esters are made by reacting a carboxylic acid and an alcohol together, with a strong acid catalyst.

- Esters are volatile, fragrant compounds used in flavourings and perfumes.

⊂◯ links

You can revise reversible reactions in 13.1 'Chemical equilibrium'.

Figure 1 Ethanoic acid reacts with carbonates to produce carbon dioxide

- Carboxylic acids dissolve in water to produce solutions with a pH value of less than 7. They have the properties typical of all acids. For example, when carboxylic acids are added to carbonates they fizz because they react to produce carbon dioxide. A salt and water are also formed in the reaction.
  For example:

  ethanoic acid + sodium carbonate → sodium ethanoate + water + carbon dioxide
  $2CH_3COOH$ + Na_2CO_3 → $2CH_3COONa$ + H_2O + CO_2

▐▐▐▶ **1** *Why do carboxylic acids have properties similar to all other acids?*

- Carboxylic acids are different from other acids because they react with alcohols in the presence of an acid catalyst to produce esters. For example, ethanol and ethanoic acid react together when mixed with sulfuric acid as a catalyst, to produce ethyl ethanoate and water:

  $$\text{ethanoic acid + ethanol} \underset{\text{sulfuric acid catalyst}}{\rightleftharpoons} \text{ethyl ethanoate + water}$$
  $$CH_3COOH + C_2H_5OH \rightleftharpoons CH_3COOC_2H_5 + H_2O$$

  In general:

  $$\text{carboxylic acid + alcohol} \underset{\text{strong acid catalyst}}{\rightleftharpoons} \text{ester + water}$$

- Esters are volatile compounds and have distinctive smells. Some esters have pleasant fruity smells and are used as flavourings and in perfumes.

▐▐▐▶ **2** *Why are some esters used as flavourings?*

- In aqueous solution, hydrochloric acid ionises completely to hydrogen ions and chloride ions.

  $$HCl(aq) → H^+(aq) + Cl^-(aq)$$

- Acids that ionise completely in aqueous solutions are known as **strong acids**.

- When ethanoic acid dissolves in water, it does not ionise completely and many of the ethanoic acid molecules remain as molecules in the solution:

  $$CH_3COOH(aq) \rightleftharpoons CH_3COO^-(aq) + H^+(aq)$$

- Acids that do not ionise completely in aqueous solution are known as **weak acids**.

- In aqueous solutions of equal concentration, weak acids have a higher pH and react more slowly than strong acids.

▐▐▐▶ **3** *Write a balanced equation to show that propanoic acid is a weak acid.*

Study tip

You should be able to explain why carboxylic acids are weak acids and know how to tell the difference between weak and strong acids.

Key words: strong acid, weak acid

1 Name and give the structural formula of the first three members of the series of alcohols.

2 Name and give the structural formula of the carboxylic acid with three carbon atoms in its molecule.

3 Draw the displayed formula of ethyl ethanoate.

4 Describe what happens when a small piece of sodium is added to some ethanol in a beaker.

5 A glass of beer containing 5% ethanol was left exposed to the air for 12 hours. The beer turned sour. Explain why.

6 Describe one reaction of ethanoic acid that is similar to the reactions of all other acids.

7 Ethanol and ethanoic acid can react together to produce an ester. Name the ester and describe the conditions used for the reaction.

8 Suggest why ethyl butanoate is added to some fruit drinks.

9 Write a word equation, and a balanced symbol equation, for the reaction of ethanoic acid, CH_3COOH, with sodium hydroxide solution, $NaOH$. The salt made in solution is sodium ethanoate, CH_3COONa.

10 Write a balanced symbol equation for the complete combustion of propanol.

11 You have been given aqueous solutions of hydrochloric acid and ethanoic acid that have the same concentration. Suggest one simple test that you could do to decide which solution is ethanoic acid.

12 Explain why hydrochloric acid is described as a strong acid whereas ethanoic acid is a weak acid.

Chapter checklist ✓ ✓ ✓

Tick when you have:

reviewed it after your lesson ✓ ☐ ☐

revised once – some questions right ✓ ✓ ☐

revised twice – all questions right ✓ ✓ ✓

Move on to another topic when you have all three ticks

Structures of alcohols, carboxylic acids and esters ☐ ☐ ☐

Properties and uses of alcohols ☐ ☐ ☐

Carboxylic acids and esters ☐ ☐ ☐

1 a Crude oil is a mixture of hydrocarbons. Crude oil is first separated into fractions before it can be used commercially.

    i What is a hydrocarbon? *(1 mark)*

    ii What do we mean by a fraction in the separation of crude oil? *(1 mark)*

    iii Name the process whereby crude oil is separated into fractions. *(1 mark)*

b The molecules in the heavier fractions can be split up into smaller, more useful molecules. A molecule of decane ($C_{10}H_{22}$) can be cracked to produce one molecule of ethene and one molecule of octane (C_8H_{18}). This is done by passing decane over powdered aluminium oxide catalyst at 500 °C.

    i What do we call the reaction in which large hydrocarbon molecules are broken down into smaller molecules? *(1 mark)*

    ii Write the balanced symbol equation for the reaction described above. *(1 mark)*

    iii What is the main use for a hydrocarbon such as octane? *(1 mark)*

    iv What is a catalyst? *(1 mark)*

    v Why is the catalyst used as a powder? *(2 marks)*

    vi Explain in detail, in terms of particles, why an increase in temperature increases the rate of this reaction. *(4 marks)*

c Ethene is used to make poly(ethene). In this reaction many molecules of ethene join together to make a large molecule. The reaction takes place in the presence of a catalyst.

    i What is the name of this type of reaction? *(1 mark)*

    ii Draw the displayed formula of ethene, showing all the chemical bonds. *(2 marks)*

    iii The displayed formula for ethane is shown below:

    Ethane will not join to other ethane molecules to form a large molecule. Suggest why ethene can react in this way but ethane cannot. *(1 mark)*

d Ethene and ethane are both colourless gases.

    Describe a chemical test that you could use to distinguish between them. *(3 marks)*

2 Vinegar is a solution that contains ethanoic acid, CH_3COOH.

a Draw the displayed formula of ethanoic acid, showing all the chemical bonds. *(1 mark)*

b Ethanoic acid reacts with sodium carbonate.

    i What would you observe during this reaction? *(1 mark)*

    ii Name all the products of the reaction between ethanoic acid and sodium carbonate. *(3 marks)*

c Ethanoic acid also reacts with sodium metal.

    i Name the gas given off in this reaction. *(1 mark)*

    ii Describe a positive test for this gas. *(2 marks)*

d Ethanoic acid can also be used to make the compound shown below:

    i What group of compounds does this molecule belong to? *(1 mark)*

    ii Name the molecule drawn above. *(1 mark)*

    iii What compound is added to ethanoic acid to make this compound? *(1 mark)*

    iv Name the other product formed in the reaction. *(1 mark)*

    v Name a catalyst used in this reaction. *(1 mark)*

    vi Give one use for the group of compounds this molecule belongs to. *(1 mark)*

Study tip

Learn the definitions of the key terms, such as 'hydrocarbon', 'alkane', 'alkene', 'cracking', 'polymer', 'monomer', 'biodegradable'.

Study tip

Remember that the rate of a chemical reaction depends on the frequency of collisions and the proportion of collisions that take place with energy greater than the activation energy of the reaction.

Study tip

You need to be able to recognise alkanes, alkenes, alcohols, carboxylic acids and esters from their structural or displayed formulae.

Exothermic and endothermic reactions

Key points

- Energy may be transferred to or from the reacting substances in a chemical reaction.

- A reaction in which energy is transferred from the reacting substances to their surroundings is called an exothermic reaction.

- In exothermic reactions, the change in enthalpy, ΔH, has a negative value.

- A reaction in which energy is transferred to the reacting substances from their surroundings is called an endothermic reaction.

- In endothermic reactions, the change in enthalpy, ΔH, has a positive value.

- When chemical reactions take place energy is transferred as bonds are broken and made. Reactions that transfer energy to the surroundings are called **exothermic** reactions. The energy transferred often heats up the surroundings and so the temperature increases.

- Exothermic reactions include:
  - combustion, such as burning fuels,
  - oxidation reactions, such as respiration, and
  - neutralisation reactions involving acids and bases.

- Scientists use the term 'enthalpy change' (given the symbol, ΔH) to describe the transfer of energy in chemical reactions at constant pressure.

- In an exothermic reaction, the products have less enthalpy content than the reactants so numerical values, measured in kilojoules per mole, are given a negative sign. For example:

$$CH_4(g) + 2O_2(g) \rightarrow CO_2(g) + 2H_2O(l) \quad \Delta H = -890\,kJ/mol$$

➧ **1** *How can you tell from observations that burning natural gas is an exothermic reaction?*

- **Endothermic** reactions take in energy from the surroundings. Some cause a decrease in temperature and others require a supply of energy. When some solid compounds are mixed with water, the temperature decreases because endothermic changes happen as they dissolve.

- **Thermal decomposition** reactions need to be heated continuously to keep the reaction going.

- In endothermic reactions, the products have more enthalpy content than the reactants so numerical values are given a positive sign. For example:

$$CaCO_3(s) \rightarrow CaO(s) + CO_2(g) \quad \Delta H = +178\,kJ/mol$$

➧ **2** *What are the two ways that show that a reaction is endothermic?*

Study tip

Remember that **exothermic** reactions involve energy EXiting (leaving) the reacting chemicals, so the surroundings get hotter.

In **endothermic** reactions energy is transferred **into** (sounds like 'endo'!) the reacting chemicals, so the surroundings get colder.

Practical

Investigating energy changes

A styrofoam cup and a thermometer can be used to investigate the energy changes in reactions.

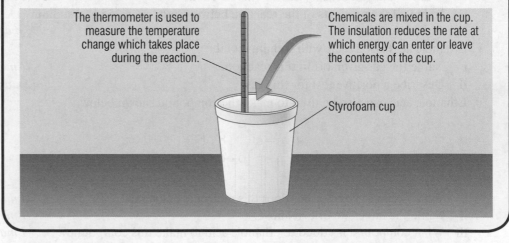

The thermometer is used to measure the temperature change which takes place during the reaction.

Chemicals are mixed in the cup. The insulation reduces the rate at which energy can enter or leave the contents of the cup.

Styrofoam cup

Key words: exothermic, endothermic, thermal decomposition

➧ **3** *State two ways in which you could make the data you collect more accurate.*

C12.2 # Using energy transfers from reactions

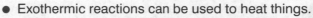

Key points

- Exothermic changes can be used in hand warmers and self-heating cans. Crystallisation of a supersaturated solution is used in reusable warmers. However, disposable, one-off warmers can give off heat for longer.

- Endothermic changes can be used in instant cold packs for sports injuries.

TO HEAT CONTAINER
Turn container UPSIDE DOWN before opening and follow instructions.

STEP 4
HOT SPOT turns from pink to white when beverage is hot. (6–8 minutes)

STEP 5
Once hot, shake 5 to 10 seconds then twist lid to align opening with pull-tab. Open and enjoy.

TWIST WHEN HOT

STEP 3
Wait 5 SECONDS and turn can right side up.

STEP 2
Place container on flat surface. Using thumb, FIRMLY push button DOWNWARD until internal foil seal tears and coloured water drains into the activation chamber.

STEP 1
PULL off tamper-proof metal bottom

Figure 2 Development of this self-heating can in the USA took about 10 years. The pink oval on the can turns white when the coffee is hot enough. This takes 6–8 minutes.

⃝ links
To revise information on reversible reactions, see 13.1 'Chemical equilibrium'.

- Exothermic reactions can be used to heat things.
- Hand warmers and self-heating cans use exothermic reactions. In some hand warmers and cans, the reactants are used up and so they cannot be used again. They use reactions such as the oxidation of iron or the reaction of calcium oxide with water. Other hand warmers use a reversible reaction such as the crystallisation of a salt. Once used, the pack can be heated in boiling water to re-dissolve the salt. These can be re-used many times.

Figure 1 A reusable hand warmer based on recrystallisation

▶ **1** *Suggest one advantage and one disadvantage of a reusable hand warmer compared with a single use hand warmer.*

- Endothermic changes can be used to cool things.
- Some chemical cold packs contain ammonium nitrate and water that are kept separated. When mixed together the ammonium nitrate dissolves and takes in energy from the surroundings. The cold pack can be used on sports injuries or to cool drinks. The reaction is reversible but not in the pack and so this type of pack can be used only once.

▶ **2** *Suggest one advantage and one disadvantage of a chemical cold pack.*

Figure 3 Instant cold packs can be applied to injuries

Study tip

You should know some examples of types of application of exothermic and endothermic reactions such as hand warmers and cold packs, but you do not need to remember the details of how they work or the reactions that are used. However, you may be asked to evaluate information that you are given about specific applications.

C12.3 Energy and reversible reactions

Key points

- In reversible reactions, the reaction in one direction is exothermic and in the other direction it is endothermic.

- In any reversible reaction, the amount of energy released when the reaction goes in one direction is exactly equal to the energy absorbed when the reaction goes in the opposite direction.

- In reversible reactions, the forward and reverse reactions involve equal but opposite energy transfers. A reversible reaction that is exothermic in one direction must be endothermic in the other direction. The amount of energy released by the exothermic reaction exactly equals the amount taken in by the endothermic reaction.

- The reaction below shows a reversible reaction where A and B react to form C and D. The products of this reaction (C and D) can then react to form A and B again.

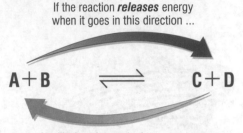

If the reaction *releases* energy when it goes in this direction ...

$$A+B \rightleftharpoons C+D$$

... it will *absorb* exactly the same amount of energy when it goes in this direction

Figure 1 A reversible reaction

- When blue copper sulfate crystals are heated the reaction is endothermic:

$$CuSO_4.5H_2O \rightleftharpoons CuSO_4 + 5H_2O$$

hydrated copper(II) sulfate (blue) $\rightleftharpoons$ **anhydrous** copper(II) sulfate (white) + water

> 1 *Why must blue copper sulfate be heated continuously to change it into anhydrous copper sulfate?*

- When water is added to anhydrous copper sulfate the reaction is exothermic.

> 2 *Why does adding water to anhydrous copper sulfate cause the mixture to get hot?*

⊂⊃ links

To revise information on reversible reactions, see 13.1 'Chemical equilibrium'.

Figure 2 Hydrated copper(II) sulfate and white anhydrous copper sulfate

Key words: hydrated, anhydrous

C12.4 Comparing the energy released by fuels

Key points

- When fuels and food react with oxygen, energy is released in an exothermic reaction. The unit of energy is the joule (but calories are still sometimes used for the energy content of foods).

- A simple calorimeter can be used to compare the energy released by different fuels or different foods in a school chemistry lab.

- We can use the equation $Q = mc\Delta T$ to calculate the amount of energy transferred from a burning fuel or food to the water in a calorimeter.

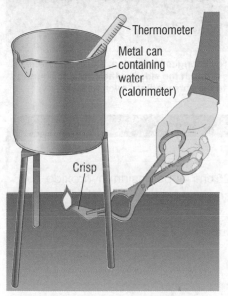

Thermometer

Metal can containing water (calorimeter)

Crisp

Figure 1 The energy released by fuels and foods when they burn can be compared using some very simple equipment

- When fuels and foods react with oxygen the reactions are exothermic. Different amounts of energy are released by different fuels and foods. The amount of energy released is usually measured in joules (J), but sometimes values are given in calories (1 cal = 4.2 J).

- We can use a calorimeter to measure the amount of energy released when substances burn. The simplest calorimeter is some water in a glass beaker or metal can. When a substance burns and heats the water, the temperature rise of the water depends on the amount of energy released.

- The amount of energy transferred to the water can be calculated using the equation:

$$Q = mc\,\Delta T$$

Where:

Q is the amount of energy transferred to the water in joules, J

m is the mass of water in grams, g

c is the specific heat capacity of water in J/g°C

ΔT is the temperature change in °C.

Study tip

Remember that you can calculate the energy released by burning a fuel using the equation $Q = mc\,\Delta T$.

You should also be able to calculate the energy released by burning a known mass of fuel in kJ/g and, when given the formula of the fuel or its relative formula mass, in kJ/mol.

Maths skills

Worked example

0.50 g of a fuel was burned and used to heat 200 g of water in a calorimeter. The temperature of the water increased by 14 °C. Find the energy released per gram of fuel burned. (The specific heat capacity of water, $c = 4.2$ J/g°C)

Using $Q = mc\,\Delta T$ Energy released = 200 × 4.2 × 14 = 11 760 J = 11.76 kJ
Energy released per g of fuel = 11.76/0.5 = 23.52 kJ/g

▶ **1** *0.45 g of fuel A was burned and heated 150 g of water in a calorimeter. The temperature of the water changed from 19 °C to 45 °C. How much energy would be released by 1.0 g of fuel?*

- Simple calorimeters do not give accurate results for the energy released because much of the energy used to heat the surroundings. However, the results can be used to compare the energy released by different fuels.

- To compare the energy released by burning different substances either the energy change in kJ per gram or the energy change in kJ per mole can be used.

- The energy change in kJ/mol can be calculated by multiplying the energy change in kJ/g by the relative formula mass of the substance.

▶ **2** *In a similar experiment to that in Question 1, fuel B released 35.6 kJ/g. The relative formula mass of fuel A is 72 and fuel B is 114. Which fuel releases more energy per mole?*

Energy transfers in solutions

- When a reaction takes place in solution, energy is transferred to or from the solution.
- We can do the reactions in an insulated container to reduce energy transfers to the surroundings.
- We can measure the temperature change of the solution and use this to calculate the energy change using the equation $Q = mc\,\Delta T$.
- In these calculations we assume the solutions behave like water. This means that 1 cm^3 of solution has a mass of 1 g and the specific heat capacity of the solution is 4.2 J/g°C.

The thermometer is used to measure the temperature change which takes place during the reaction.

The temperature change in reactions such as those when solids are added to aqueous solutions can be measured, e.g. in displacement or neutralisation reactions. The insulated cup reduces the rate of energy transfer to or from the surroundings.

Polystyrene cup

Figure 1 A simple calorimeter can be used to measure energy changes in solution. The polystyrene is a good thermal insulator so helps to reduce energy transfer through the sides of the container during reactions. A lid on the calorimeter reduces energy transfer to the surroundings even further.

Maths skills

Worked example

A student added 25 cm^3 of dilute nitric acid to 25 cm^3 of potassium hydroxide solution in a polystyrene cup. He recorded a temperature rise of 12 °C. Calculate the energy change.

$$Q = mc\,\Delta T \qquad \text{Volume of solution} = 25 + 25 = 50\ cm^3$$

$$\text{Energy change} = 50 \times 4.2 \times 12$$
$$= 2520\,J = 2.52\,kJ$$

> **1** *When 50 cm^3 of sulfuric acid was added to 100 cm^3 of sodium hydroxide in a polystyrene cup the temperature increased by 12 °C. Calculate the energy change.*

- When a solid is added to water or to an aqueous solution we assume that the volume of the solution does not change. We also assume that 1 cm^3 of solution has a mass of 1 g and that its specific heat capacity is 4.2 J/g°C.
- If we know the number of moles involved in the reaction for which we have calculated the energy change, we can calculate the energy change for the reaction in kJ/mol.

> **2** *When 5.6 g of iron filings reacted completely with 200 cm^3 of copper(II) sulfate solution the temperature of the solution increased by 17 °C. Calculate the energy change in kJ/mol of iron.*
> *(Relative atomic mass of Fe = 56)*

C12.6 Energy level diagrams

Key points

- We can show the relative difference in the energy of reactants and products on energy level diagrams.
- Catalysts provide a pathway with a lower activation energy so the rate of reaction increases.
- Bond breaking is endothermic and bond making is exothermic.

Study tip

Learn how to sketch and label energy level diagrams for exothermic and endothermic reactions and show the effect of a catalyst on the activation energy.

- We can show the energy changes for chemical reactions on energy level diagrams.
- The difference between the energy levels of reactants and products is the energy change for the reaction.
- The energy level diagram for an exothermic reaction is shown on the left.

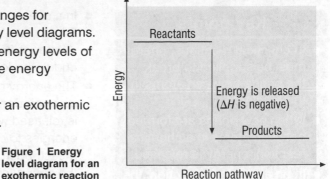

Figure 1 Energy level diagram for an exothermic reaction

▶ **1** *Draw a similar energy level diagram for an endothermic reaction.*

- During a chemical reaction bonds in the reactants must be broken for the reaction to happen. Breaking bonds is endothermic because energy is taken in.
- The minimum energy needed for the reaction to happen is called the **activation energy**.
- When new bonds in the products are formed, energy is released and so this is exothermic.
- We can show the activation energy and how the energy changes during a reaction on an energy level diagram. This type of diagram is shown below.

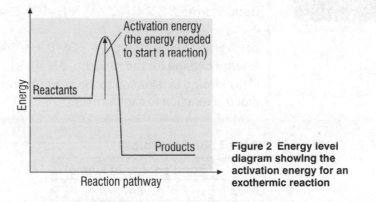

Figure 2 Energy level diagram showing the activation energy for an exothermic reaction

▶ **2** *Draw a similar energy level diagram for an endothermic reaction.*

- Catalysts increase the rate of a reaction by providing a different pathway with an activation energy that is lower. The effect of a catalyst on an exothermic reaction is shown below.

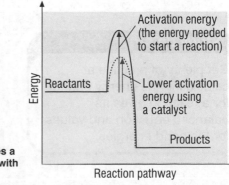

Figure 3 A catalyst provides a different reaction pathway with a lower activation energy

⚭ links

To revise more about the enthalpy change, ΔH, in chemical reactions look back at 12.1 'Exothermic and endothermic reactions'.

Key word: activation energy

▶ **3** *Draw an energy level diagram to show the effect of a catalyst on an endothermic reaction.*

C12.7 # Bond dissociation energy calculations

Key points

- In chemical reactions, energy must be supplied to break the bonds between atoms in the reactants.

- When new bonds are formed between atoms in a chemical reaction, energy is released.

- In an exothermic reaction, the energy released when new bonds are formed is greater than the energy absorbed when bonds are broken.

- In an endothermic reaction, the energy released when new bonds are formed is less than the energy absorbed when bonds are broken.

- We can calculate the overall energy change in a chemical reaction using bond energies.

- In a chemical reaction, energy is needed to break the bonds in the reactants. Energy is released when new bonds are formed in the products. It is the difference in these energy changes that makes the overall reaction exothermic or endothermic.

- The energy needed to break the bond between two atoms is called the **bond dissociation energy** (or bond energy) for that bond. An equal amount of energy is released when the bond forms between two atoms and so we can use bond energies to calculate the overall energy change for a reaction. Bond energies are measured in kJ/mol. The balanced equation for the reaction is needed to calculate the energy change for a reaction. Then calculate:

  – the total amount of energy needed to break all of the bonds in the reactants
  – the total amount of energy released in making all of the bonds in the products
  – the difference between the two totals.

Maths skills

Worked example

Use the bond energies in the table below to calculate the energy change for burning methane:

$$CH_4 + 2O_2 \rightarrow CO_2 + 2H_2O$$

Bonds broken: $4 \times$ C—H + $2 \times$ O=O   Energy needed = $(4 \times 413) + (2 \times 498)$
$$= +2648\,kJ$$

Bonds formed: $2 \times$ C=O + $4 \times$ H—O   Energy released = $(2 \times 805) + (4 \times 464)$
$$= -3466\,kJ$$

So overall energy change = $+2648 + (-3466) = -818\,kJ$

Energy change for the reaction, $\Delta H = -818\,kJ/mol$

(This energy is released to the surroundings as the negative sign of ΔH tell us that the reaction is exothermic)

Table of bond energies

Bond	Bond energy in kJ/mol
C—C	347
C—H	413
H—O	464
O=O	498
C=O	805

Study tip

Get plenty of practice at calculating the energy change for a reaction given its balanced equation and values for the bond energies.

▶ **1** *Calculate the energy change for burning propane using the bond energies in the table:*

$$C_3H_8 + 5O_2 \rightarrow 3CO_2 + 4H_2O$$

Key word: bond dissociation energy

1. What is meant by the 'activation energy' of a reaction?

2. Name two types of reaction that are exothermic.

3. Why must calcium carbonate be heated continuously to convert it into calcium oxide and carbon dioxide?

4. Why do simple calorimeters give inaccurate results for the energy released by burning a fuel?

5. How can you tell from an energy level diagram that a reaction is endothermic?

6. Draw an energy level diagram for the exothermic reaction $CH_4 + 2O_2 \rightarrow CO_2 + 2H_2O$. Show and label the reaction pathway, the activation energy and the energy change of the reaction.

7. 0.50 g of a fuel was burned and heated 200 g of water in a calorimeter. The temperature increased by 15 °C.

    Calculate the energy released by the fuel using the equation $Q = mc\Delta T$, in which $c = 4.2 \, J/g\,°C$

8. 0.10 mol of zinc was added to 100 cm³ of copper(II) sulfate solution. The temperature increased by 18 °C. Use the equation $Q = mc\Delta T$ to calculate the energy change for the reaction in kJ/mol.

9. 100 cm³ of hydrochloric acid containing 0.10 mol of HCl was added to 100 cm³ of sodium hydroxide solution containing 0.10 mol of NaOH. The temperature of the solution increased by 7 °C. Calculate the energy change for this reaction in kJ/mol.

10. Draw and label an energy level diagram with reaction pathways to show the effect of a catalyst on an exothermic reaction.

11. Calculate the energy change for the reaction $CH_2{=}CH_2 + 3O_2 \rightarrow 2CO_2 + 2H_2O$ using bond energies: C—H = 413 kJ/mol, C=C = 612 kJ/mol, O=O = 498 kJ/mol, C=O = 805 kJ/mol, H—O = 464 kJ/mol.

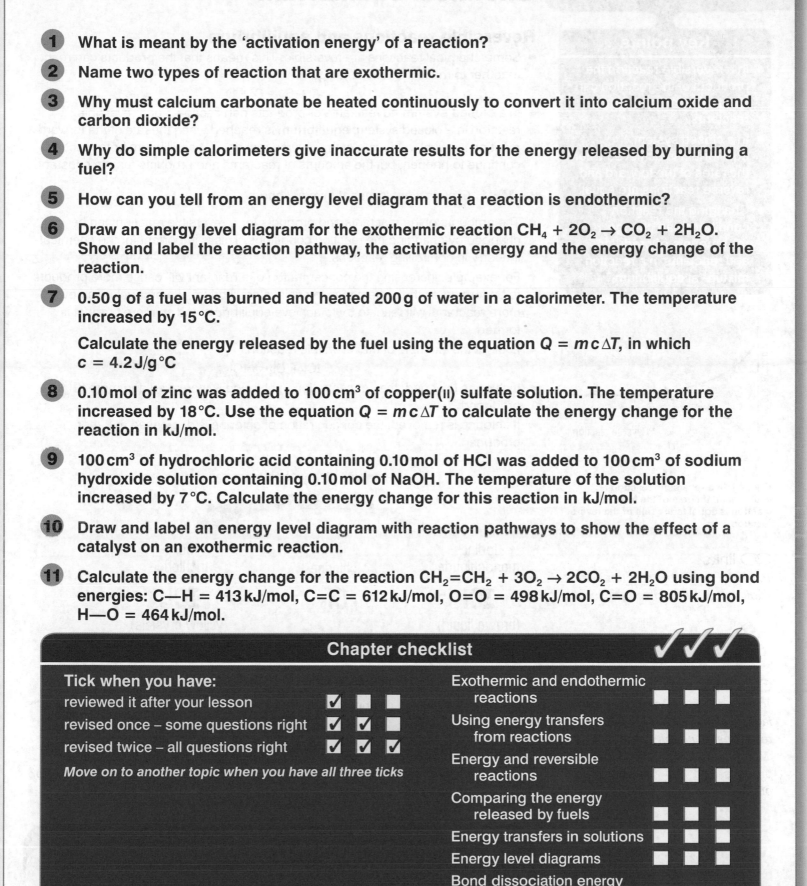

Chapter checklist			✓ ✓ ✓

Tick when you have:

reviewed it after your lesson ☑ ☐ ☐

revised once – some questions right ☑ ☑ ☐

revised twice – all questions right ☑ ☑ ☑

Move on to another topic when you have all three ticks

Exothermic and endothermic reactions ☐ ☐ ☐

Using energy transfers from reactions ☐ ☐ ☐

Energy and reversible reactions ☐ ☐ ☐

Comparing the energy released by fuels ☐ ☐ ☐

Energy transfers in solutions ☐ ☐ ☐

Energy level diagrams ☐ ☐ ☐

Bond dissociation energy calculations ☐ ☐ ☐

Chemical equilibrium

Reversible reactions and equilibrium

- Some chemical reactions are reversible. This means that the products can react together to make the reactants again:

$$A + B \rightleftharpoons C + D$$

- In a **closed system** no reactants or products can escape. For a reversible reaction in a closed system, **equilibrium** is reached when the rate of the forward reaction is equal to the rate of the reverse reaction. At equilibrium both reactions continue to happen, but the amounts of reactants and products remain constant.

▶ 1 *Explain what is meant by equilibrium.*

- The amounts of the reactants and products for a reversible reaction can be changed by changing the reaction conditions. This is important for the chemical industry in controlling reactions.

- For example, increasing the concentration of a reactant will cause more products to be formed as the system tries to achieve equilibrium. If a product is removed, more reactants will react to try to achieve equilibrium and so more product is formed.

- Look at the example of the reversible reaction:

$$ICl + Cl_2 \rightleftharpoons ICl_3$$

- If chlorine is added, the concentration of chlorine is increased and more ICl_3 is produced.

- If chlorine is removed, the concentration of chlorine is decreased and more ICl is produced.

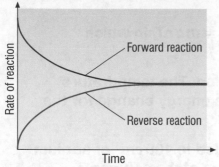

Figure 1 In a reversible reaction at equilibrium, the rate of the forward reaction is equal to the rate of the reverse reaction

∞ links

To revise reversible reactions, look back at 2.5 'Reversible reactions'.

∞ links

To revise the economic and safety factors associated with reversible reactions in industry, see 13.3 'Making ammonia – the Haber process' and 13.4 'The economics of the Haber process'.

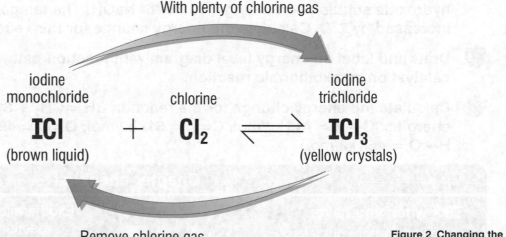

Figure 2 Changing the equilibrium mixture

▶ 2 *To make SO₃, the reaction $2SO_2(g) + O_2(g) \rightleftharpoons 2SO_3(g)$ is done in a reactor over a heated catalyst. Why is the SO₃ removed from the reactor as soon as it is made?*

Study tip

It is the rates of the forward and reverse reactions that are equal at equilibrium, not the amounts of reactants and products. However, the amounts of reactants and products remain constant when the reaction is at equilibrium.

Key words: closed system, equilibrium

Altering conditions

Key points

- Pressure can affect reversible reactions involving gases at equilibrium. Increasing the pressure favours the reaction that forms fewer molecules of gas. Decreasing the pressure favours the reaction with the greater number of molecules of gas formed.

- We can change the amount of products formed at equilibrium by changing the temperature at which we carry out a reversible reaction.

- Increasing the temperature favours the endothermic reaction. Decreasing the temperature favours the exothermic reaction.

○○ links

Revise energy changes in reversible reactions in 12.3 'Energy and reversible reactions'.

Study tip

Even though there are two reactions in a reversible reaction, by convention when we write an equation for any reaction we call the substances on the left-hand side the reactants and those on the right-hand side the products. In the exams you will be told in which direction the reaction is exothermic or endothermic.

Changing pressure

- If we change the conditions of a system at equilibrium, the position of equilibrium shifts as if to try to cancel out the change.
- For reversible reactions that have different numbers of molecules of gases on one side of the equation than the other, changing the pressure will affect the position of equilibrium.
- For example, if the pressure is increased, the position of equilibrium will shift to try to reduce the pressure (favouring the reaction that produces fewer molecules of gas). This is summarised in the table:

If the forward reaction produces **more** molecules of gas …	If the forward reaction produces **fewer** molecules of gas …
… an increase in pressure decreases the amount of products formed.	… an increase in pressure increases the amount of products formed.
… a decrease in pressure increases the amount of products formed.	… a decrease in pressure decreases the amount of products formed.

- For example: in the reversible reaction: $2NO_2(g) \rightleftharpoons N_2O_4(g)$ there are more gaseous reactant molecules than gaseous product molecules. Therefore increasing the pressure will increase the amount of N_2O_4 (product) in the mixture at equilibrium.

▷ **1** *For the reaction $2SO_2(g) + O_2(g) \rightleftharpoons 2SO_3(g)$, what change in pressure will increase the amount of SO_3 in the equilibrium mixture?*

Changing temperature

- Reversible reactions are exothermic in one direction and endothermic in the other direction.
- Increasing the temperature favours the reaction in the endothermic reaction. The equilibrium shifts as if to lower the temperature by taking in energy.
- Decreasing the temperature favours the exothermic reaction. This is summarised in the table:

If the forward reaction is **exothermic** …	If the forward reaction is **endothermic** …
… an increase in temperature decreases the amount of products formed.	… an increase in temperature increases the amount of products formed.
… a decrease in temperature increases the amount of products formed.	… a decrease in temperature decreases the amount of products formed.

- For example: for the reversible reaction: $2NO_2(g) \rightleftharpoons N_2O_4(g)$ the forward reaction is exothermic, so increasing the temperature will produce more NO_2 (reactant) in the mixture at equilibrium.

▷ **2** *The reaction $2SO_2(g) + O_2(g) \rightleftharpoons 2SO_3(g)$ is exothermic in the forward direction. What change in temperature will increase the amount of SO_3 at equilibrium?*

Student Book
pages 164–165 **C13.3**

Making ammonia – the Haber process

- The Haber process is used to manufacture ammonia, which can be used to make fertilisers and other chemicals.
- Nitrogen from the air and hydrogen, which is usually obtained from natural gas, are purified and mixed in the correct proportions.
- The gases are passed over an iron catalyst at a temperature of about 450°C and a pressure of about 200 atmospheres.
- These conditions are chosen to give a fast rate of reaction and a reasonable yield of ammonia.
- The reaction is reversible: $N_2(g) + 3H_2(g) \rightleftharpoons 2NH_3(g)$

1 *Write a word equation for the manufacture of ammonia.*

- Some of the ammonia that is produced breaks down into nitrogen and hydrogen and the yield of ammonia is only about 15%.
- The gases that come out of the reactor are cooled so the ammonia condenses. The liquid ammonia is separated from the unreacted gases. The unreacted gases are recycled so they are not wasted.

2 *What is done in the Haber process to conserve raw materials?*

Student Book
pages 166–167 **C13.4**

The economics of the Haber process

Why is there an optimum pressure for the Haber process?

- In the Haber process nitrogen and hydrogen react to make ammonia in a reversible reaction:

$$N_2(g) + 3H_2(g) \rightleftharpoons 2NH_3(g)$$

- The products have fewer molecules of gas than the reactants, so the higher the pressure is, the greater the yield of ammonia. However, the higher the pressure is, the more energy is needed to compress the gas. Higher pressures also need stronger reaction vessels and pipes which increases costs.
- A pressure of about 200 atmospheres is often used as a compromise between the costs and the yield.

1 *Why do higher pressures increase the costs of an industrial process?*

Why is there an optimum temperature for the Haber process?

- The forward reaction is exothermic and so the lower the temperature is, the greater the yield of ammonia. However, the reaction rate decreases as the temperature is lowered and the iron catalyst becomes ineffective so it would take a longer time to produce any ammonia.
- Therefore, a compromise temperature of about 450°C is usually used to give a reasonable yield in a short time.

2 *At a temperature of 100°C and 200 atmospheres pressure the yield of ammonia is 98%. Why is the Haber process not done at this temperature?*

1 What does the sign $\rightleftharpoons$ signify in a reaction?

2 Explain why a reversible reaction carried out under closed conditions will reach a state of equilibrium.

3 What effect will removing chlorine gas have on the equilibrium mixture shown below:

$$ICl(l) + Cl_2(g) \rightleftharpoons ICl_3(s)$$

4 Explain the effect of increasing the pressure on the equilibrium mixture shown in question 3?

5 The reaction $CaCO_3(s) \rightleftharpoons CaO(s) + CO_2(g)$ reaches equilibrium in a closed system. The forward reaction is endothermic. How could the amount of calcium oxide produced by the reaction be increased?

6 Ammonia is made by the Haber process. The equation for the reaction is:

$$N_2(g) + 3H_2(g) \rightleftharpoons 2NH_3(g)$$

a What are the raw materials used for the process?

b What conditions are used in the Haber process?

c How is ammonia separated from the unreacted nitrogen and hydrogen?

7 The forward reaction shown in the chemical equation for the Haber process in question 6 is exothermic.
Explain why the Haber process is carried out at a temperature of about 450°C.

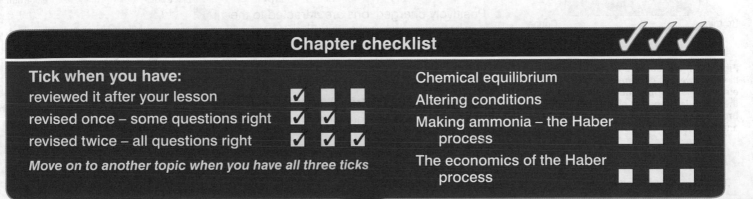

Chapter checklist				✓	✓	✓
Tick when you have:				Chemical equilibrium	☐ ☐ ☐	
reviewed it after your lesson	✓	☐	☐	Altering conditions	☐ ☐ ☐	
revised once – some questions right	✓	✓	☐	Making ammonia – the Haber process	☐ ☐ ☐	
revised twice – all questions right	✓	✓	✓			
Move on to another topic when you have all three ticks				The economics of the Haber process	☐ ☐ ☐	

C14.1

Electrolysis

DOUBLE AWARD

- Electrolysis is the process that uses electricity to break down ionic compounds into elements.

- When electricity is passed through a molten ionic compound or a solution containing ions, electrolysis takes place.

- The substance that is broken down is called the **electrolyte**.

⟱➤ **1** *What must be done to ionic compounds before they can be electrolysed?*

- The electrical circuit has two electrodes that make contact with the electrolyte.

- The electrodes are often made of an **inert** substance that does not react with the products.

- The positive electrode is called the **anode**. The negative electrode is called the **cathode**.

- The ions in the electrolyte move to the electrodes where they are discharged to produce elements.

Demonstration

The electrolysis of molten lead bromide

This demonstration needs a fume cupboard because bromine is toxic and corrosive.

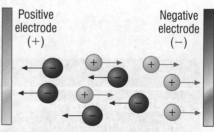

Figure 1 Passing electricity through molten lead bromide. It forms molten lead and brown bromine gas as the electrolyte is broken down by the electricity.

⟱➤ **2** *What is observed at a) the anode (positive electrode), and b) the cathode (negative electrode)?*

- Electrolysis breaks down lead bromide into lead and bromine:

  lead bromide → lead + bromine
  $$PbBr_2(l) \rightarrow Pb(l) + Br_2(g)$$

- Positively charged ions are attracted to the cathode (negative electrode) where they form metals or hydrogen, depending on the ions in the electrolyte.

- Negatively charged ions are attracted to the anode (positive electrode) where they lose their charge to form non-metallic elements.

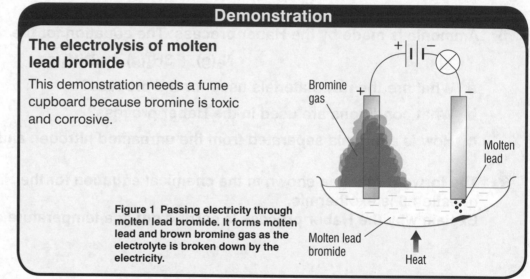

Figure 3 An ion always moves towards the oppositely charged electrode

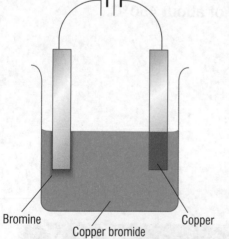

Figure 2 If we dissolve copper bromide in water, we can decompose it by electrolysis. Copper metal is formed at the cathode (negative electrode). Brown bromine appears in solution around the anode (positive electrode).

Key words: electrolyte, inert, anode, cathode

⟱➤ **3** *Molten zinc chloride is electrolysed. Name the substances produced a) at the anode (positive electrode), and b) at the cathode (negative electrode).*

C14.2 Changes at the electrodes

Key points

- Negative ions lose electrons and so are oxidised at the anode (positive electrode).
- Positive ions gain electrons and so are reduced at the cathode (negative electrode).
- When aqueous solutions are electrolysed, oxygen gas is produced at the anode (positive electrode) unless the solution contains halide ions.
- When aqueous solutions are electrolysed, hydrogen gas is produced at the cathode (negative electrode) unless the solution contains ions of a metal that is less reactive than hydrogen.

⚭ links

To revise more about reduction and oxidation in terms of electron transfer, look back to 7.2 'Displacement reactions'.

- When positively charged ions reach the cathode (negative electrode) they gain electrons to become neutral atoms.
- Gaining electrons is called **reduction**, so the positive ions have been reduced. Ions with a single positive charge gain one electron and those with a 2+ charge gain two electrons.
- At the anode (positive electrode), negative ions lose electrons to become neutral atoms. This is **oxidation**. Some non-metal atoms combine to form molecules, for example bromine forms Br_2.

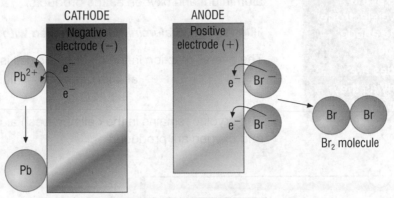

Figure 1 Changes at the electrodes in the electrolysis of molten lead bromide

⟱ 1 *What type of change happens at the cathode (negative electrode) when sodium ions become sodium atoms?*

Half equations

- We can represent the changes at the electrodes by **half equations**. The half equations for lead bromide are:
  At the cathode (negative electrode): $Pb^{2+} + 2e^- \rightarrow Pb$
  At the anode (positive electrode): $2Br^- \rightarrow Br_2 + 2e^-$

⟱ 2 *Complete the half equation for the formation of chlorine at an anode:*
$2Cl^- \rightarrow \ldots + \ldots$

- Water contains hydrogen ions, $H^+(aq)$, and hydroxide ions, $OH^-(aq)$.
- When aqueous solutions of ions are electrolysed, hydrogen may be produced at the cathode (negative electrode). This happens if the other positive ions in the solution are those of a metal more reactive than hydrogen, such as in the electrolysis of a solution of a potassium compound. Hydrogen is less reactive than potassium, so hydrogen gas is given off at the cathode, not potassium.
- At the anode (positive electrode), oxygen is usually produced from aqueous solutions. However, if the solution contains a reasonably high concentration of a halide ion, then a halogen will be produced.

⟱ 3 *Name the products at a) the anode (positive electrode) and b) the cathode (negative electrode) when aqueous copper sulfate solution is electrolysed using carbon electrodes.*

Study tip

Oxidation and reduction reactions don't have to involve oxygen. More generally they involve the transfer of electrons. Remember OILRIG – **O**xidation **I**s **L**oss (of electrons), **R**eduction **I**s **G**ain (of electrons).

Key words: reduction, oxidation, half equations

C14.3   The extraction of aluminium

Key points

- Aluminium oxide, from the ore bauxite, is electrolysed to manufacture aluminium.
- The aluminium oxide is mixed with molten cryolite to lower its melting point.
- Aluminium forms at the cathode (negative electrode) and oxygen at the anode (positive electrode).
- The carbon anodes are replaced regularly as they gradually burn away.

- Aluminium is more reactive than carbon and so it must be extracted from its ore by electrolysis.
- Its ore, bauxite, contains aluminium oxide which must be purified and then melted so that it can be electrolysed.
- Aluminium oxide melts at over 2000 °C, which would need a lot of energy. Aluminium oxide is mixed with another ionic compound called cryolite, so that the mixture melts at about 850 °C.
- The mixture can be electrolysed at this lower temperature and produces aluminium and oxygen as the products.

⮕ **1** *Why is aluminium oxide mixed with cryolite in the electrolysis cell?*

- The overall reaction in the electrolysis cell is:

$$\text{aluminium oxide} \rightarrow \text{aluminium} + \text{oxygen}$$
$$2Al_2O_3(l) \rightarrow 4Al(l) + 3O_2(g)$$

- The cryolite remains in the cell and fresh aluminium oxide is added as aluminium and oxygen are produced.

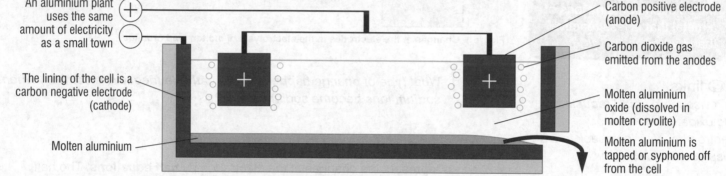

An aluminium plant uses the same amount of electricity as a small town

The lining of the cell is a carbon negative electrode (cathode)

Molten aluminium

Carbon positive electrode (anode)

Carbon dioxide gas emitted from the anodes

Molten aluminium oxide (dissolved in molten cryolite)

Molten aluminium is tapped or syphoned off from the cell

Figure 1 A cell used in the extraction of aluminium by electrolysis

- At the cathode (negative electrode) aluminium ions are reduced to aluminium atoms by gaining electrons. The molten aluminium metal is collected from the bottom of the cell.
- At the anode (positive electrode) oxide ions are oxidised to oxygen atoms by losing electrons and the oxygen atoms form oxygen molecules.

⮕ **2** *What are the products formed at each electrode in the electrolysis cell?*

Half equations

- At the cathode (negative electrode): $Al^{3+}(l) + 3e^- \rightarrow Al(l)$
- At the anode (positive electrode): $2O^{2-}(l) \rightarrow 2O_2(g) + 4e^-$
- The anodes used in the cell are made of carbon. At the high temperature of the cell the oxygen reacts with the carbon anodes to produce carbon dioxide gas. This means that the carbon anodes gradually burn away and so they have to be replaced regularly.

Study tip

You do not need to know the formula of cryolite, just that it is used to lower the operating temperature of the electrolysis cell to make it possible to electrolyse aluminium oxide and to save energy.

C14.4 Electrolysis of brine

Key points

- When we electrolyse brine we get three products – chlorine gas, hydrogen gas and sodium hydroxide solution (an alkali).
- Chlorine is used to make bleach, which kills bacteria, and to make plastics.
- Hydrogen is used to make margarine.
- Sodium hydroxide is used to make bleach, paper and soap.

Practical

Electrolysing brine in the lab

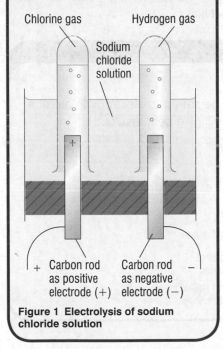

Figure 1 Electrolysis of sodium chloride solution

⊂⊃ links

To revise what happens when two ions are attracted to an electrode, look back to 14.2 'Changes at the electrodes'.

- Brine is a solution of sodium chloride in water. The solution contains sodium ions, $Na^+(aq)$, chloride ions, $Cl^-(aq)$, hydrogen ions, $H^+(aq)$, and hydroxide ions, $OH^-(aq)$.
- When we electrolyse brine hydrogen is produced at the cathode (negative electrode) from the hydrogen ions. Chlorine is produced at the anode (positive electrode) from the chloride ions. This leaves an alkaline solution of sodium ions and hydroxide ions, $NaOH(aq)$.

Half equations

- The half equations for the reactions at the electrodes are:
  - At the anode (positive electrode): $2Cl^- \rightarrow Cl_2 + 2e^-$
  - At the cathode (negative electrode): $2H^+ + 2e^- \rightarrow H_2$

⫸ **1** *Why is hydrogen produced when sodium chloride solution is electrolysed?*

⫸ **2 a** *How can you positively test for the gases collected?*
   b *The solution near the cathode (negative electrode) was tested with universal indicator solution. What happens and what does this tell us?*

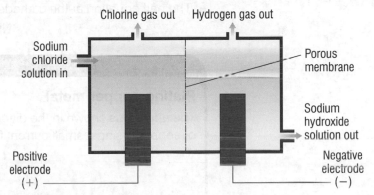

Figure 2 The industrial electrolysis of brine (sodium chloride solution)

- The electrolysis of brine (sodium chloride solution) is an important chemical process in industry.
- Sodium hydroxide is a strong alkali and has many uses including making soap, making paper, making bleach, neutralising acids and controlling pH.
- Chlorine is used to kill bacteria in drinking water and in swimming pools, and to make bleach, disinfectants and plastics.
- Hydrogen is used to make margarine and hydrochloric acid.

⫸ **3** *Why is the electrolysis of brine an important industrial process?*

C14.5 # Electroplating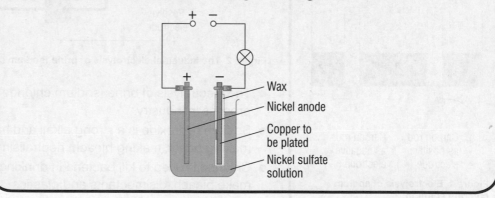

DOUBLE AWARD

Key points

- We can electroplate objects to improve their appearance, protect their surface, and to use smaller amounts of precious metals.
- The object to be electroplated is made the cathode (negative electrode) in an electrolysis cell. The plating metal is made the anode (positive electrode). The electrolyte contains ions of the plating metal.

- Electroplating uses electrolysis to put a thin coating of metal onto an object. Gold, silver and chromium plating are often used. We can electroplate objects for several reasons that may include:
  - to make the object look more attractive
  - to protect a metal object from corroding
  - to increase the hardness of a surface
  - to reduce costs by using a thin layer of an expensive metal instead of the pure metal.

�▶ **1** *Why are some knives, forks and spoons silver plated?*

- For electroplating, the object to be plated is used as the cathode (negative electrode). The anode (positive electrode) is made from the plating metal. The electrolyte is a solution containing ions of the plating metal.
- At the anode (positive electrode), atoms of the plating metal lose electrons to form metal ions which go into the solution.
  - The half equation at the nickel anode is:

$$Ni(s) \rightarrow Ni^{2+}(aq) + 2e^-$$

- At the cathode (negative electrode), metal ions from the solution gain electrons to form metal atoms which are deposited on the object to be plated.
- The half equation at the cathode (which is the metal object to be plated) is:

$$Ni^{2+}(aq) + 2e^- \rightarrow Ni(s)$$

Practical

Plating copper metal

The apparatus shown in the diagram below can be set up to electroplate a piece of copper. Using a small current for a long time will give best results.

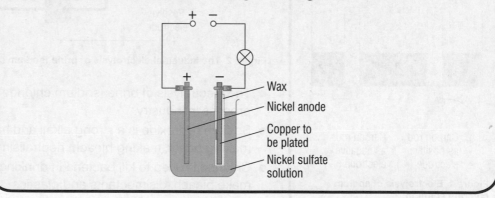

Wax

Nickel anode

Copper to be plated

Nickel sulfate solution

▶ **2** *What happens at the negative electrode in the experiment above?*

▶ **3** *Describe how you would silver plate a small piece of copper jewellery.*

Study tip

For electroplating, the anode (positive electrode) is not inert – it produces ions of the metal used to plate the object.

1. Name the products at the anode and cathode when the following molten salts are electrolysed:

   a calcium chloride

   b lithium iodide

   c lead bromide

2. Name the products at each electrode when the following concentrated solutions are electrolysed:

   a copper chloride solution

   b potassium bromide solution

3. Name the three products when sodium chloride solution is electrolysed in industry and give one use for each.

4. Aluminium is extracted from aluminium oxide, Al_2O_3, which is inexpensive.

   a Why is extracting aluminium an expensive process?

   b Why is cryolite used in the process to extract aluminium?

5. In the extraction of aluminium, write half equations for the reactions at the a) cathode, and b) anode.

6. Explain as fully as you can what happens at the electrodes when molten sodium chloride is electrolysed.

7. Write half equations for the reactions at the electrodes when magnesium chloride solution $MgCl_2$(aq) is electrolysed using carbon electrodes.

8. Why are some items of jewellery made of gold-plated nickel?

9. Write half equations for the reactions at:

   a the anode, and

   b the cathode,

   in the process of nickel-plating a metal object.

Chapter checklist		✓ ✓ ✓
Tick when you have:	Electrolysis	☐ ☐ ☐
reviewed it after your lesson ☑ ☐ ☐	Changes at the electrodes	☐ ☐ ☐
revised once – some questions right ☑ ☑ ☐	The extraction of aluminium	☐ ☐ ☐
revised twice – all questions right ☑ ☑ ☑	Electrolysis of brine	☐ ☐ ☐
Move on to another topic when you have all three ticks	Electroplating	☐ ☐ ☐

Tests for positive ions

Key points

- Most Group 1 and Group 2 metal ions can be identified using flame tests.
- Sodium hydroxide solution can be used to identify different metal ions, depending on the precipitate that is formed.

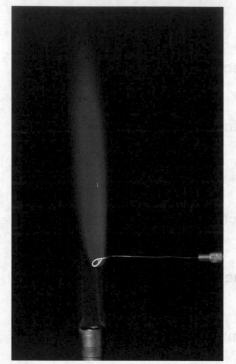

Figure 1 Flame test colour of lithium ions

- Some positive ions can be identified using a flame test or by testing with sodium hydroxide solution.
- Some metal ions produce colours when put into a non-luminous Bunsen burner flame:

Metal ion	Flame colour
Lithium (Li$^+$)	crimson
Sodium (Na$^+$)	yellow
Potassium (K$^+$)	lilac
Calcium (Ca^{2+})	brick red
Barium (Ba^{2+})	apple green

▐▐▶ **1** *Which metal ions give reddish colours in a flame?*

- The hydroxides of most metals that have ions with 2+ and 3+ charges are insoluble in water. When **sodium hydroxide solution is added** to solutions of these ions, a precipitate of the metal hydroxide forms.
- Aluminium, calcium and magnesium ions all form white precipitates of their hydroxides. For example, with a solution containing magnesium chloride:

$$MgCl_2(aq) + 2NaOH(aq) \rightarrow Mg(OH)_2(s) + 2NaCl(aq)$$
$$\text{white precipitate}$$

- The ionic equation for the reaction of aqueous hydroxide ions with a solution containing aluminium ions is:

$$Al^{3+}(aq) + 3OH^-(aq) \rightarrow Al(OH)_3(s)$$

- When excess sodium hydroxide solution is added the precipitate of aluminium hydroxide dissolves, showing aluminium ions are present. We can distinguish calcium ions from magnesium ions by a flame test – calcium ions will give a brick red flame whereas magnesium ions do not colour the flame.
- Copper(II) hydroxide is blue.

$$Cu^{2+}(aq) + 2OH^-(aq) \rightarrow Cu(OH)_2(s)$$

- Iron(II) hydroxide is green.

$$Fe^{2+}(aq) + 2OH^-(aq) \rightarrow Fe(OH)_2(s)$$

- Iron(III) hydroxide is brown.

$$Fe^{3+}(aq) + 3OH^-(aq) \rightarrow Fe(OH)_3(s)$$

▐▐▶ **2** *A few drops of sodium hydroxide solution were added to a colourless solution and a white precipitate appeared. When excess sodium hydroxide was added the precipitate remained. Which metal ions could be present?*

Study tip

Both lithium ions and calcium ions give red flame colours. Lithium ions give a brighter red but it is difficult to tell them apart from this single test. Testing solutions of the ions with sodium hydroxide solution will show which is which because calcium ions will give a white precipitate but lithium ions will not.

You should be able to write balanced symbol equations, as well as ionic equations, for the reactions of metal ions that give precipitates with sodium hydroxide solution.

C15.2 # Tests for negative ions

Key points

- We identify carbonates by adding dilute acid, which produces carbon dioxide gas. The gas turns limewater cloudy.
- We identify halides by adding nitric acid, then silver nitrate solution. This produces a precipitate of silver halide:
  – chloride = white,
  – bromide = cream,
  – iodide = pale yellow.
- We identify sulfates by adding hydrochloric acid, then barium chloride solution. This produces a white precipitate of barium sulfate.

⚭ links

To revise more about carbonates, look back to 6.4 'Metal carbonates'.

There are three tests for negative ions that you need to know.

- **Carbonate ions**: Add dilute hydrochloric acid to the substance to see if it fizzes. If it does and the gas produced turns limewater cloudy, the substance contains carbonate ions.

For example, if the carbonate is potassium carbonate, the reaction we get with dilute hydrochloric acid is:

$$K_2CO_3(s) + 2HCl(aq) \rightarrow 2KCl(aq) + H_2O(l) + CO_2(g)$$

We can represent the reaction of the carbonate ion with dilute acid by just showing the ions that change in the reaction in an ionic equation:

$$\underset{\text{acid}}{2H^+(aq)} + \underset{\text{carbonate ion}}{CO_3^{2-}(s)} \rightarrow CO_2(g) + H_2O(l)$$

▶ **1** *Which gas turns limewater cloudy?*

- **Halide ions**: Add dilute nitric acid and then silver nitrate solution:
  – chloride ions give a white precipitate
  – bromide ions give a cream precipitate
  – iodide ions give a yellow precipitate.

For example, if the unknown halide was lithium chloride, the precipitation reaction would be:

$$LiCl(aq) + AgNO_3(aq) \rightarrow LiNO_3(aq) + AgCl(s)$$

Here is the ionic equation, where X^- is the halide ion:

$$Ag^+(aq) + X^-(aq) \rightarrow AgX(s)$$

Figure 1 Precipitates of silver chloride, silver bromide and silver iodide

▶ **2** *Why must you add nitric acid and not hydrochloric acid or sulfuric acid when testing with silver nitrate solution for halides?*

- **Sulfate ions**: Add dilute hydrochloric acid and then barium chloride solution. If a white precipitate forms, sulfate ions are present.

If the unknown compound was sodium sulfate, then the equation for the precipitation reaction would be:

$$Na_2SO_4(aq) + BaCl_2(aq) \rightarrow 2NaCl(aq) + BaSO_4(s)$$

Here is the ionic equation:

$$Ba^{2+}(aq) + SO_4^{2-}(aq) \rightarrow BaSO_4(s)$$

Study tip

Make sure you learn these tests – many candidates lose marks because they do not know the tests or their results.

Figure 2 The white precipitate of barium sulfate

C15.3

Separating mixtures

Key points

- A mixture is made up of two or more elements or compounds which are not chemically combined together.

- Mixtures can be separated by physical means, such as filtration, crystallisation and distillation.

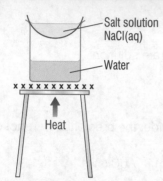

Figure 2 Crystallising sodium chloride from its solution in water

- A **mixture** is made up of two or more elements or compounds which are not chemically combined together.

- The substances in a mixture can be separated from each other by physical means. The techniques available include:
  - filtration   – crystallisation
  - distillation   – chromatography

Filtration

- We use **filtration** to separate substances that are insoluble in a particular solvent from those that are soluble.

> 1 *When you mix sulfur powder and copper sulfate with water and filter, what is the a) residue, and b) the filtrate in the experiment?*

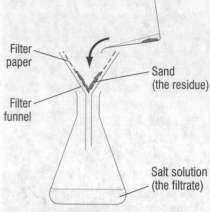

Figure 1 Filtering a mixture of sand, salt and water in the lab

Crystallisation

- We use **crystallisation** to separate a dissolved solid from a solution.

Distillation

- **Distillation** allows us to collect the solvent from a solution or to separate miscible liquids with different boiling points. (Miscible liquids will dissolve in each other and do not form separate layers).

- The solvent is boiled off from the solution. The vapour is passed through a condenser to cool the vapour. The vapour condenses so that the pure liquid can be collected.

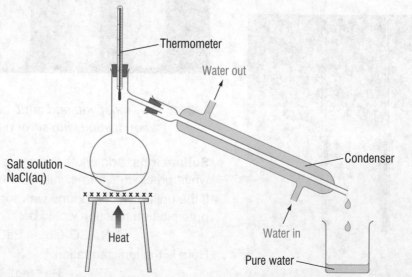

Figure 3 Distilling pure water from a salt solution. A vertical fractionating column can be inserted above the flask, before the condenser, to improve separation of miscible liquids with similar boiling points. This is called fractional distillation as opposed to the simple distillation shown above.

> 2 *What part of the distillation apparatus cools down vapours?*

⦾ links

To revise about crystallisation look back to 6.2 'Making salts from metals or insoluble bases' and 6.3 'Neutralisation, precipitation and making salts'.

Key words: mixture, filtration, crystallisation, distillation

Paper chromatography

Key points

- Scientists can analyse unknown substances in solution by using paper chromatography.
- R_f values can be measured and matched against databases to identify specific substances.
- Modern instrumental techniques provide fast, accurate and sensitive ways of analysing chemical substances.

- Scientists have many instruments to identify unknown compounds. Some of these are more sensitive, automated versions of techniques used in school labs, such as paper **chromatography**.
- Paper chromatography can be used to analyse the artificial colours in food or the dyes in inks.
- A spot of colour is put onto paper and a solvent is allowed to move through the paper.
- The colours move different distances depending on their solubility.

▐▐▐▶ **1** *What method can be used to analyse food colourings?*

Practical

Detecting dyes in food colourings or inks

In this experiment you can make a chromatogram to analyse various food colourings or inks.

The experiment is set up as shown:

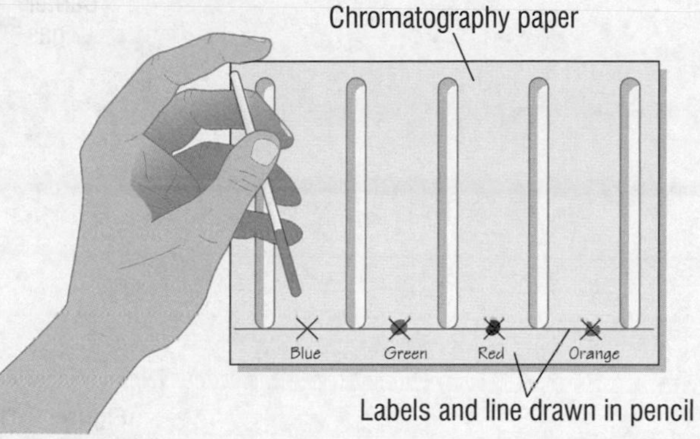

Figure 1 Setting up a chromatogram

Chromatography paper

Blue   Green   Red   Orange

Labels and line drawn in pencil

∞ links

To revise information about the instruments used by chemists to analyse substances, see 15.5 'Instrumental analysis'.

▐▐▐▶ **2** *What can you deduce from your chromatogram?*

- Once the compounds in a mixture have been separated using chromatography, they can be identified.
- We can compare the chromatogram with others obtained from known substances, as long as the same solvent at the same temperature has been used.
- The data is presented as an R_f (**retention factor**) value. This is a ratio, calculated by:

$$R_f = \frac{\text{the distance a spot travels up the paper}}{\text{the distance the solvent front travels}}$$

- Here is how to calculate an R_f value from a chromatogram obtained from an experiment (see Figure 2 opposite):
  The R_f value of A = 8/12 = 0.67
  The R_f value of B = 3/12 = 0.25

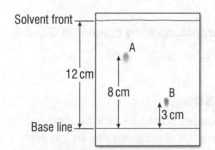

Figure 2 The R_f value of an unknown substance, in a particular solvent at a given temperature, can be compared with values in a database to identify the substance

- Modern instrumental methods have some benefits over older methods, such as they are highly accurate and sensitive; they are quicker; they enable very small samples to be analysed.
- Against this, the main disadvantages of using instrumental methods are that the equipment is usually very expensive, takes special training to use, and gives results that can often be interpreted only by comparison with data from known substances.

Key words: chromatography, R_f (retention factor)

C15.5 # Instrumental analysis

Key points

- Compounds in a mixture can be separated using gas chromatography.
- Once separated, compounds can be identified using a mass spectrometer.
- The mass spectrometer can be used to find the relative molecular mass of a compound from its molecular ion peak shown on its mass spectrum.

- Samples for analysis are often mixtures that we need to separate so that the compounds can be identified. One way of doing this is to use **gas chromatography** linked to a **mass spectrometer** (GC–MS).
- In gas chromatography the mixture is carried by a gas through a long column packed with particles of a solid. The individual compounds travel at different speeds through the column and come out at different times. The amount of substance leaving the column at different times is recorded against time and shows the number of compounds in the mixture and their **retention times**. The retention times can be compared with the results for known compounds to help identify the compounds in the mixture.

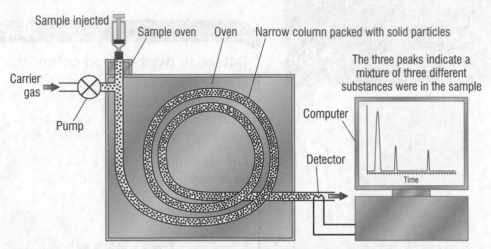

Figure 1 This is the apparatus used for gas chromatography. The gas chromatograph produced on the computer screen is a mixture of three different substances. There was more of substance A than B or C in the sample mixture. Also, as substance A was first to leave the column, it had the weakest attraction for the solid packed in the column.

- The output from the gas chromatography column can be linked directly to a mass spectrometer (GC–MS). The mass spectrometer gives further data that a computer can use quickly to identify the individual compounds by matching against the mass spectra of known substances.

▶ **1** *What is the main purpose of the gas chromatography column in GC–MS analysis?*

Measuring relative molecular masses

- A mass spectrometer can give the relative molecular mass of a compound. For an individual compound the peak with the largest mass corresponds to an ion with just one electron removed. This peak is called the **molecular ion peak** and is furthest to the right on a mass spectrum.

▶ **2** *How is the relative molecular mass shown in a mass spectrum?*

Key words: gas chromatography, mass spectrometer, retention time, molecular ion peak

1. Write an ionic equation to show aqueous iron(III) ions reacting with hydroxide ions in solution.

2. What colour in a flame test will positively identify barium present in a compound?

3. What is the positive test for the presence of sulfate ions in a compound?

4. When sodium hydroxide solution was added to an unknown solution a green precipitate formed. When hydrochloric acid and barium chloride solution were added to another sample of the unknown solution a white precipitate formed. Which ions were in the unknown solution?

5. A compound gave a lilac colour in a flame test. Nitric acid and silver nitrate solution were added to a solution of the compound and a yellow precipitate was formed. Name the compound.

6. Dilute hydrochloric acid was added to a green compound. The mixture gave off a gas that turned limewater cloudy and a blue solution was formed. When sodium hydroxide solution was added to the blue solution a blue precipitate was produced. Name the green compound.

7. What substances in foods can be detected by paper chromatography?

8. On a paper chromatogram, a spot was obtained from an unknown substance 5 cm above the baseline. The solvent front was measured at 20 cm above the baseline. What is the R_f value of this substance?

9. What information can be obtained from the molecular ion peak in a mass spectrum?

10. What do we call the separation technique used to obtain a sample of potassium chloride from its aqueous solution?

11. How would you separate sand from a mixture of sand and copper sulfate?

12. Explain how you can get pure water from a sample of seawater.

Chapter checklist	✓	✓	✓
Tick when you have:			
reviewed it after your lesson	✓	☐	☐
revised once – some questions right	✓	✓	☐
revised twice – all questions right	✓	✓	✓
Move on to another topic when you have all three ticks			

Tests for positive ions	☐	☐	☐
Tests for negative ions	☐	☐	☐
Separating mixtures	☐	☐	☐
Paper chromatography	☐	☐	☐
Instrumental analysis	☐	☐	☐

1 a The electrolysis of brine (sodium chloride solution) is an important industrial process.

The diagrams below show two experiments set up during an investigation of the electrolysis of sodium chloride.

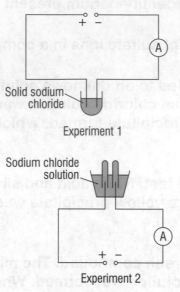

Experiment 1

Experiment 2

   i   What would be the reading on the ammeter in Experiment 1?   (1 mark)
   ii Explain your answer.   (2 marks)
   iii A student wanted to try electrolysing molten sodium chloride. Discuss the problems with this idea.   (5 marks)

b The equations below show the reactions which take place in Experiment 2.
   What is missing in each equation?

   i $H_2O(l) \rightleftharpoons H^+(aq) + \underline{\hspace{1cm}} (aq)$
   ii $2H^+(aq) + 2e^- \rightarrow \underline{\hspace{1cm}} (g)$
   iii $2Cl^-(aq) \rightarrow Cl_2(g) + \underline{\hspace{1cm}}$ (3 marks)
   iv Which substance provides the aqueous hydrogen ions?   (1 mark)
   v   Name the product formed at the anode.   (1 mark)
   vi Name the product formed at the cathode.   (1 mark)

c Name a suitable material for the electrodes in Experiment 2.   (1 mark)

d Explain what you would expect to observe when universal indicator solution is added to the solution in Experiment 2 near the cathode.   (4 marks)

e *In this question you will be assessed on using good English, organising information clearly and using specialist terms where appropriate.*

   We can also use electrolysis to electroplate a metal object. Describe and explain how you would electroplate a metal key with nickel. (The formula of the nickel ion is Ni^{2+}).

   Include in your answer:
   A fully labelled circuit diagram
   Half equations for the reactions taking place at each electrode.
   An explanation of how the electroplating process works.   (6 marks)

2 A chemist was given the task of identifying an unknown white powder. Here are the positive results from the laboratory tests carried out.

Test 1 – a flame test produced a bright yellow flame

Test 2 – a white precipitate was formed on addition of dilute hydrochloric acid and barium chloride solution.

a i What can be concluded from Test 1? *(1 mark)*

ii What can be concluded from Test 2? *(1 mark)*

iii Write the chemical formula of the unknown white powder analysed. *(1 mark)*

The chemist was given another unknown compound to test and the results are shown below:

Test 3 – a white precipitate was formed on addition of sodium hydroxide solution

Test 4 – a flame test was negative

Test 5 – a cream precipitate was formed when tested with dilute nitric acid and silver nitrate solution.

b i Name two possible compounds that could give the results in Tests 3–5. *(2 marks)*

ii Describe how you could test which of these two possibilities is the correct identity of the unknown compound tested. *(3 marks)*

c We can also use analytical instruments to test unknown substances.

i Give two advantages of using modern instrumental analysis compared with traditional laboratory tests. *(2 marks)*

ii One technique used to identify unknown compounds is gas chromatography linked to mass spectroscopy (GC-MS). Why is the gas chromatography used before the sample of unknown material is passed into a mass spectrometer? *(1 mark)*

iii In an analysis, the following mass spectrum was obtained:

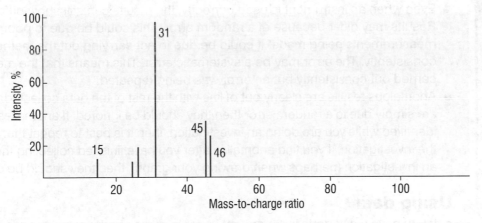

What does this tell us about the unknown compound? *(3 marks)*

Experimental data handling

Student Book
pages 194–203

Key points

- Plan investigations to produce repeatable, reproducible and valid results. Take care to ensure fair testing.

- Careful use of the correct equipment can improve accuracy. The mean of a repeat set of readings is the sum of the values divided by how many values there are.

- Human error can produce random and systematic errors. Examine anomalous results and discard them if necessary.

- The reproducibility of data can be checked by looking at similar work done by others, by using a different method or by others checking your method.

Study tip

Trial runs will tell you a lot about how your investigation might work out. They should get you to ask yourself:

- Do you have the correct conditions?
- Have you chosen a sensible range?
- Have you got readings that are close together?
- Will you need to repeat your readings?

Study tip

When you draw a results table, put the independent variable in the first column, and the dependent variable in the other column(s). When you draw a graph, plot the independent variable along the horizontal axis and the dependent variable up the vertical axis.

Investigations

- The **independent variable** is the one you choose to vary in your investigation.
- The **dependent variable** is used to judge the effect of varying the independent variable.
- A fair test is one in which only the independent variable affects the dependent variable. All other variables are controlled and kept constant if at all possible. (In fieldwork, the best you can do is to make sure that each of the many control variables change in much the same way).
- If you are investigating two variables in a large population then you will need to do a survey. Again, it is impossible to control all of the variables. So here, the larger the sample size tested, the more valid the results will be.
- Variables can be one of two different types:
  - A **categoric variable** is one that is best described by a label (usually a word). The type of metal is a categoric variable, e.g. magnesium or zinc.
  - A **continuous variable** is one that we measure, so its value could be any number.
- When you are designing an investigation you must make sure that others can repeat any results you get – this makes it **reproducible**. You should also plan to make each result **repeatable**. You can do this by getting consistent sets of repeat measurements.
- You must also make sure you are measuring the actual thing you want to measure. You need to make sure that you have controlled as many other variables as you can, so that no-one can say that your investigation is not **valid**.
- A precise set of repeat readings is grouped closely together.
- An accurate set of results will have a mean (average) close to the true value.

Setting up investigations

- Even when an instrument is used correctly, the results can still show differences. Results may differ because of a random error. This could be due to poor measurements being made. It could be due to not carrying out the method consistently. The error may be a systematic error. This means that the method was carried out consistently but an error was being repeated.
- Anomalous results are clearly out of line with the rest of the data collected. If they are simply due to a random error then they should be ignored. If anomalies can be identified while you are doing an investigation, then it is best to repeat that part of the investigation. If you find anomalies after you have finished collecting the data for an investigation (perhaps when drawing your graph), then they should be discarded.

Using data

- If you have a categoric independent variable and a continuous dependent variable then you should use a bar chart to display your data.
- If you have a continuous independent and a continuous dependent variable then use a line graph.
- If you are still uncertain about a conclusion, you could check reproducibilty by:
  - looking for other similar work on the internet or from others in your class
  - getting somebody else to redo your investigation
  - trying an alternative method to see if you get the same results.
- You will find Paper 2-style questions designed to test your understanding of practical skills included in the pages of Examination-style questions in this Revision Guide.

Key words: reproducible, repeatable, valid

Question

Bromine water can be used to test how unsaturated vegetable oils are. The greater the number of double bonds in the hydrocarbon chains in the plant oils, the more bromine water is needed to react completely with the oil. Different cooking oils were tested. A student carried out two titrations with each oil. Bromine water was added from a burette to each oil and swirled in a conical flask. The volume added before the mixture in the flask stayed yellow was noted.

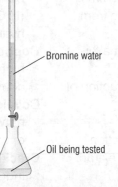

Bromine water

Oil being tested

The results are in this table:

Type of oil	Volume of bromine water added (cm³)	
	Test 1	**Test 2**
Oilio	24.2	24.9
Sunoil	17.8	16.0
Palmio	7.9	7.1
Vegoil	13.0	12.9
Cooklite	17.9	17.4

1 (a) How can you make the judgement of the colour change at the end point as accurate as possible in each individual test carried out?

Put the flask with the oil in on a piece of white paper.

(1)

1 (b) Why is each test repeated?

To make it a fair test.

(1)

1 (c) Are there any anomalous results? Explain how you decided?

Yes, with Sunoil there is a big difference between Test 1 and Test 2.

(1)

1 (d) Which results show the greatest precision?

Vegoil because the two results are very close together.

(1)

1 (e) Explain how might the accuracy of the results be improved?

Do more tests with each oil and take the average.

(2)

This answer gains 1 mark. This would make it easier to see a colour change (but a white tile is a better practical suggestion).

No marks – repeats are carried out to improve the accuracy of the mean calculated. Fair testing involves controlling variables e.g. using the same volume of each oil in all the titrations – but repeatability is not about fair testing.

No marks – this answer refers to precision, i.e. the range within a set of repeat readings. The answer is Oilio because the first test in a titration is a rough guide and usually too much solution is added from the burette. However with Oilio, Test 2 was the larger volume of bromine water added – different from the results of the other four oils.

This answer gains 1 mark. It is correct as the range of repeat readings is smallest.

This answer gains 1 mark. More repeat readings gets a mark. The second mark is for explaining that in titrations you are looking for two concordant readings for accuracy (i.e. two identical titres). The second mark would also be given for saying that with more repeats you could identify anomalous results and discard them before calculating a mean value.

Glossary

Acid: When dissolved in water, its solution has a pH number less than 7. Acids are proton (H^+ ion) donors.

Activation energy: The minimum energy needed to start off a reaction.

Alkali: Its solution has a pH number greater than 7.

Alkali metal: Elements in Group 1 of the periodic table, e.g. lithium (Li), sodium (Na), potassium (K).

Alkane: Saturated hydrocarbon with the general formula C_nH_{2n+2}, for example methane, ethane and propane.

Alkene: Unsaturated hydrocarbon which contains a carbon–carbon double bond. The general formula is C_nH_{2n}, for example ethene C_2H_4.

Alloy: A mixture of metals (sometimes with non-metals). For example, brass is a mixture of copper and zinc.

Aluminium: A low density, corrosion-resistant metal used in many alloys, including those used in the aircraft industry.

Amphoteric oxides: These oxides behave like both acids and bases e.g. aluminium oxide.

Anode: The positive electrode in an electrolysis cell.

Anhydrous: Describes a substance that does not contain water.

Aqueous solution: The mixture made by adding a soluble substance to water.

Atmosphere: The relatively thin layer of gases that surround planet Earth.

Atom: The smallest part of an element that can still be recognised as that element.

Atomic number: The number of protons (which equals the number of electrons) in an atom. It is sometimes called the proton number.

Base: The oxide, hydroxide or carbonate of a metal that will react with an acid, forming a salt as one of

the products. (If a base dissolves in water it is called an alkali). Bases are proton (H^+ ion) acceptors.

Biodegradable: Materials that can be broken down by microorganisms.

Biodiesel: Fuel for cars made from plant oils.

Biofuel: Fuel made from animal or plant products.

Bioleaching: Process of extraction of metals from ores using microorganisms.

Blast furnace: The huge reaction vessels used in industry to extract iron from its ore.

Bond energy: The energy needed to break a particular chemical bond.

Burette: A long glass tube with a tap at one end and markings to show volumes of liquid, used to add precisely known amounts of liquids to a solution in a conical flask below it

Calcium carbonate: The main compound found in limestone. It is a white solid whose formula is $CaCO_3$.

Carbon monoxide: A toxic gas with the formula CO.

Cast iron: The impure iron taken directly from a blast furnace.

Catalyst: A substance that speeds up a chemical reaction. At the end of the reaction the catalyst remains chemically unchanged.

Cathode: The negative electrode in an electrolysis cell.

Cement: A building material made by heating limestone and clay.

Chromatography: The process whereby small amounts of dissolved substances are separated by running a solvent along a material such as absorbent paper.

Closed system: A system in which no matter or energy enters or leaves.

Collision theory: An explanation of chemical reactions in terms of reacting particles colliding with

sufficient energy for a reaction to take place.

Compound: A substance made when two or more elements are chemically bonded together. For example, water (H_2O) is a compound made from hydrogen and oxygen.

Copper-rich ore: Rock that contains a high proportion of a copper compound.

Covalent bonding: The attraction between two atoms that share one or more pairs of electrons.

Cracking: The reaction used in the oil industry to break down large hydrocarbons into smaller, more useful ones. This occurs when the hydrocarbon vapour is either passed over a hot catalyst or mixed with steam and heated to a high temperature.

Crystallisation: A technique used to separate a dissolved crystalline solid from its solution.

Delocalised electron: Bonding electron that is no longer associated with any one particular atom.

Desalination: The removal of salts from water (usually seawater) to make it suitable for drinking and other uses.

Diffusion: The process whereby the particles in liquids or gases mix with each other due to the random motion of the particles

Displace: When one element takes the place of another in a compound. For example, iron + copper sulfate → iron sulfate + copper.

Distillation: Separation of a liquid from a mixture by evaporation followed by condensation.

Dot-and-cross diagram: A drawing to show the arrangement of the outer shell electrons only of the atoms or ions in a substance.

Double bond: A covalent bond made by the sharing of two pairs of electrons.

Electrolysis: The breakdown of a substance containing ions by electricity.

Electrolyte: A liquid, containing free moving ions, that is broken down by electricity in the process of electrolysis.

Electron: A tiny particle with a negative charge. Electrons orbit the nucleus in atoms or ions.

Electronic structure: A set of numbers to show the arrangement of electrons in their shells (or energy levels), for example, the electronic structure of a potassium atom is 2,8,8,1.

Element: A substance made up of only one type of atom. An element cannot be broken down chemically into any simpler substance.

Empirical formula: The simplest ratio of elements in a compound.

End point: The point in a titration where the reaction is complete and titration should stop.

Endothermic: A reaction that takes in energy from the surroundings.

Energy level: see Shell.

Equilibrium: The point in a reversible reaction in which the forward and backward rates of reaction are the same. Therefore, the amounts of substances present in the reacting mixture remain constant.

Ethene: An alkene with the formula C_2H_4.

Exothermic: A reaction that gives out energy to the surroundings.

Fermentation: The reaction in which the enzymes in yeast turn glucose into ethanol and carbon dioxide.

Filtration: The technique used to separate substances that are insoluble in a particular solvent from those that are soluble.

Flammable: Easily ignited and capable of burning rapidly.

Fluoridation: The addition of fluoride to drinking water supplies to help prevent tooth decay.

Fraction: Hydrocarbons with similar boiling points separated from crude oil.

Fractional distillation: A way to separate liquids from a mixture of liquids by boiling off the substances at different temperatures, then condensing and collecting the liquids.

Fullerene: Form of the element carbon that can form a large cage-like structure, based on hexagonal rings of carbon atoms.

Functional group: An atom or group of atoms that give organic compounds their characteristic reactions.

Gas: The state of matter in which there are large spaces, on average, between particles that are moving randomly at high speeds.

Gas chromatography: The process of separating the components in a mixture by passing the vapours through a column and detecting them as they leave the column at different times.

Giant covalent structure: A huge 3-D network of covalently bonded atoms (e.g. the giant lattice of carbon atoms in diamond or graphite).

Giant lattice: A huge 3-D network of atoms or ions (e.g. the giant ionic lattice of sodium chloride).

Giant structure: See giant lattice.

Global dimming: The reflection of sunlight by tiny solid particles in the air.

Global warming: The increasing of the average temperature of the Earth.

Gradient: Change of the quantity plotted on the y-axis divided by the change of the quantity plotted on the x-axis.

Group: All the elements in each column (labelled 1 to 7 and 0) down the periodic table.

Half equation: An equation that describes reduction (gain of electrons) or oxidation (loss of electrons), such as the reactions that take place at the electrodes during electrolysis. For example:
$$Na^+ + e^- \rightarrow Na.$$

Halides: Salts containing ions of the Group 7 elements

Halogens: The elements found in Group 7 of the periodic table.

Homologous series: A group of related organic compounds that have the same functional group, e.g. the molecules of the homologous series of alcohols all contain the −OH group.

Hydrated: Describes a substance that contains water in its crystals, e.g. hydrated copper sulfate.

Hydrocarbon: A compound containing only hydrogen and carbon.

Incomplete combustion: When a fuel burns in insufficient oxygen, producing carbon monoxide as a toxic product.

Inert: Unreactive.

Intermolecular force: The attraction between the individual molecules in a covalently bonded substance.

Ion: A charged particle produced by the loss or gain of electrons from an atom.

Ionic equation: An equation that shows only ions or atoms that change in a chemical reaction.

Ion-exchange column: A water softener that works by replacing calcium and magnesium ions with sodium or hydrogen ions, removing the hardness.

Ionic bonding: The electrostatic force of attraction between positively and negatively charged ions.

Isotopes: Atoms that have the same number of protons but different numbers of neutrons, i.e. they have the same atomic number but different mass numbers.

Lattice: A giant three-dimensional network of particles.

Limewater: The common name for calcium hydroxide solution.

Liquid: The state of matter in which the particles are touching but can slip and slide over and around each other in random motion

Macromolecule: Giant covalent structure.

Mass number: The number of protons plus neutrons in the nucleus of an atom.

Mass spectrometer: A machine that can be used to analyse small amounts of a substance to identify it and to find its relative molecular mass.

Mixture: When some elements or compounds are mixed together and intermingle but do not react together (i.e. no new substance is made). A mixture is not a pure substance.

Mole: The amount of substance in the relative atomic or formula mass of a substance in grams.

Molecular formula: The chemical formula that shows the actual numbers of atoms in a particular molecule (e.g. C_2H_4).

Molecular ion peak: The peak on the mass spectrum of a substance which tells us the relative molecular mass of the substance. The peak is produced by the heaviest positive ion shown on the mass spectrum.

Monomers: Small reactive molecules that react together in repeating sequences to form a very large molecule (a polymer).

Nanoscience: The study of very tiny particles or structures between 1 and 100 nanometres in size – where 1 nanometre = 10^{-9} metres.

Neutral: A solution with a pH value of 7 that is neither acidic nor alkaline. Alternatively, something that carries no overall electrical charge – neither positively nor negatively charged.

Neutralisation: The chemical reaction of an acid with a base forming a salt and water. If the base is a carbonate or hydrogen carbonate, carbon dioxide is also produced in the reaction.

Neutron: A dense particle found in the nucleus of an atom. It is electrically neutral, carrying no charge.

Nitrogen oxides: Gaseous pollutants given off from motor vehicles; a cause of acid rain.

Noble gases: The very unreactive elements found in Group 0 of the periodic table.

Nucleus: The very small and dense central part of an atom which contains protons and neutrons.

Ore: Rock which contains enough metal to make it economically worthwhile to extract the metal.

Oxidation: The reaction when oxygen is added to a substance (or when electrons are lost).

Oxidised: A reaction where oxygen is added to a substance (or when electrons are lost from a substance).

Particulate: Small solid particle given off from motor vehicles as a result of incomplete combustion of its fuel.

Percentage yield: The actual mass of product collected in a reaction divided by the maximum mass that could have been formed in theory, multiplied by 100.

Periodic table: An arrangement of elements in the order of their atomic numbers, forming groups and periods.

pH scale: A scale of numbers (0–14) that shows how strongly acidic or alkaline a solution is. Acids have a pH value of less than 7 (pH 1 is strongly acidic). Alkalis have a pH value above 7 (pH 14 is strongly alkaline). A neutral liquid has a pH value of 7.

Phytomining: The process of extraction of metals from ores using plants.

Pipette: A glass tube used to measure accurate volumes of liquids.

Polymer: Very large molecules made up of many repeating units, for example, poly(ethene).

Polymerisation : The reaction of monomers to make a polymer.

Precipitate: An insoluble solid formed by a reaction taking place in solution.

Product: A substance made as a result of a chemical reaction.

Propene: An alkene with the formula C_3H_6.

Proton: A tiny positive particle found inside the nucleus of an atom.

Reactant: A substance we start with before a chemical reaction takes place.

Reactivity series: A list of elements in order of their reactivity. The most reactive element is put at the top of the list.

Reduction: A reaction in which oxygen is removed (or electrons are gained).

Relative atomic mass, A_r: The average mass of the atoms of an element compared with carbon-12 (which is given a mass of exactly 12). The average mass must take into account the proportions of the naturally occurring isotopes of the element.

Relative formula mass, M_r: The total of the relative atomic masses, added up in the ratio shown in the chemical formula, of a substance.

Retention factor, R_f: On a paper chromatogram, this is a ratio, calculated by dividing the distance a spot travels up the paper by the distance the solvent front travels.

Retention time: The time it takes a component in a mixture to pass through the column during gas chromatography.

Reversible reaction: A reaction in which the products can re-form the reactants.

Rusting: The corrosion of iron by reaction with oxygen and water to form rust (hydrated iron(III) oxide).

Sacrificial protection: A method of protection against rusting by connecting to, or adding a thin coating of, a metal which is more reactive than iron, such as zinc or magnesium.

Salt: A salt is a compound formed when some or all of the hydrogen in an acid is replaced by a metal (or by an ammonium ion). For example, potassium nitrate, KNO_3 (from nitric acid).

Saturated hydrocarbon: Describes a hydrocarbon that contains as many hydrogen atoms as possible in each molecule.

Shape memory alloy: Mixture of metals which respond to changes in temperature.

Shell (or energy level): An area in an atom, around its nucleus, where the electrons are found.

Smart polymer: Polymers that change in response to changes in their environment.

Smelting: Heating a metal ore in order to extract its metal.

Solid: The state of matter in which the particles are packed tightly together and vibrate about fixed positions.

Stainless steel: A chromium–nickel alloy of steel which does not rust.

State symbol: The abbreviations used in balanced symbol equations to show if reactants and products are solid (s), liquid (l), gas (g) or dissolved in water (aq).

States of matter: solid, liquid and gas are three states of matter.

Steel: An alloy of iron with small amounts of carbon or other metals, such as nickel and chromium, added.

Strong acids: Acids that ionise completely in aqueous solutions.

Sulfur dioxide: A toxic gas whose formula is SO_2. It causes acid rain.

Thermal decomposition: The breakdown of a compound by heat.

Thermosetting polymer: Polymer that can form extensive cross-linking between chains, resulting in rigid materials which are heat-resistant.

Thermosoftening polymer: Polymer that forms plastics which can be softened by heat, then remoulded into different shapes as they cool down and set.

Titanium: A shiny, corrosion-resistant metal used to make alloys.

Titration: A method for measuring the volumes of two solutions that react together.

Transition element: Element from the central block of the periodic table. It has typical metallic properties and forms a coloured compound.

Transition metal: See Transition element.

Universal indicator: A mixture of indicators which can change through a range of colours depending on the pH of a solution. Its colour is matched to a pH number using a pH scale. It shows how strongly acidic or alkaline liquids and solutions are.

Unsaturated hydrocarbon: A hydrocarbon whose molecules contain at least one carbon–carbon double bond.

Viscosity: The resistance of a liquid to flowing or the 'thickness' or resistance of a liquid to pouring.

Weak acids: Acids that do not ionise completely in aqueous solutions.

Yield: See Percentage yield.

Answers

1 Fundamental ideas (1)

1.1
1 Gas
2 Freezing/solidifying and condensing/condensation

1.2
1 We can smell the perfume/aftershave at a distance from the bottle but we cannot see any substance moving through the air to us, suggesting the existence of particles too small to be seen with the naked eye.
2 Hydrogen chloride, as its particles travel a shorter distance down the tube and we know that small, light particles diffuse faster than large, heavy ones.
3 Because the particles of a liquid move around more slowly than those in a gas and there is less space between the particles.

1.3
1 Elements
2 An atom of hydrogen
3 A compound

1.4
1 Equal numbers of protons and electrons
2 13 protons, 13 electrons, 14 neutrons

1.5
1 Diagram: three concentric circles with dot or Al at centre, innermost circle with 2 electrons (dots or crosses), next with 8 electrons, outer circle with 3 electrons.
2 Both have 5 electrons in highest energy level (outer shell).

1.6
1 The mass of an electron is very small compared to that of a proton or neutron.
2 9 protons, 9 electrons, 10 neutrons
3 Atoms of the same element (or atoms with the same atomic/proton number) that have different numbers of neutrons (different mass numbers).

Answers to end of Chapter 1 questions

1 Energy absorbed – boiling, melting
  Energy released – condensing, freezing
2 They vibrate about a fixed point
3 Diffusion
4 Elements: Ca, H_2, Ne, O_2; Compounds: CH_4, HCl, MgO, SO_2
5 11 protons, 11 electrons, 12 neutrons
6 In order of atomic numbers (proton numbers)
7 Diagram: three concentric circles with a dot or S at centre, innermost circle with 2 electrons (dots or crosses), next circle with 8 electrons, outer circle with 6 electrons.
8 Both have 3 (same number of) electrons in their highest energy level (outer shell).
9 Subtract the atomic number from the mass number.
10 a Isotopes
   b $^{35}_{17}Cl$ has two fewer neutrons than $^{37}_{17}Cl$ (18 neutrons compared with 20 neutrons).

2 Fundamental ideas (2)

2.1
1 23 g
2 It has (two main) isotopes and the relative atomic mass is an average value.
3 $(23 \times 2) + 32 + (16 \times 4) = 142$
4 $24 + 12 + (16 \times 3) = 84 g$ (must have g)

2.2
1 $(12/16) \times 100 = 75\%$
2 $70/56 = 1.25 : 30/16 = 1.875$, $1 : 1.5$, $2 : 3$, empirical formula Fe_2O_3

2.3
1 Magnesium reacts with hydrochloric acid to produce magnesium chloride and hydrogen; one atom of magnesium reacts with two molecules of hydrochloric acid to give one magnesium ion and two chloride ions and one molecule of hydrogen.
2 a $H_2 + Cl_2 \rightarrow 2HCl$
  b $4Na + O_2 \rightarrow 2Na_2O$
  c $Na_2CO_3 + 2HCl \rightarrow 2NaCl + H_2O + CO_2$

2.4
1 $CaCO_3 = 100$, $CaO = 56$, one mole $CaCO_3$ gives one mole of CaO or 100 g $CaCO_3$ gives 56 g CaO, 10 g $CaCO_3$ gives $(10/100) \times 56 = 5.6$ g

2.5
1 A reaction that can go both forwards and backwards, or both ways or in both directions.

2.6
1 $2Ca + O_2 \rightarrow 2CaO$, 80 g $Ca \rightarrow 112$ g CaO, 4 g $Ca \rightarrow 5.6$ g CaO, $(4.4/5.6) \times 100 = 78.6\%$
2 Reactions may not go to completion, other reactions may happen, some product may be lost when separated or collected.
3 To help conserve resources, reduce waste and/or pollution.

Answers to end of Chapter 2 questions

1 8.8 g
2 Reversible
3 ammonium chloride → ammonia + hydrogen chloride
   $NH_4Cl(s)$ → $NH_3(g)$ + $HCl(g)$
4 a lead nitrate + potassium iodide → potassium nitrate + lead iodide
  b two potassium atoms/ions, two nitrogen atoms, six oxygen atoms, one lead atom/ion, two iodine atoms/iodide ions
5 62
6 102 g
7 51.4% (51%)
8 Two from: magnesium oxide was lost or not collected, the magnesium did not all react, magnesium reacted with other substances in air, magnesium was not pure.
9 V_2O_5
10 13.6 g
11 75%

Answers to Examination-style questions

1 a $2Li(s) + Cl_2(g) \rightarrow 2LiCl(s)$ (2)
  b i 3 protons (1)
      and 3 electrons (1)
    ii Diagram of lithium atom – two circles drawn, with 2 electrons in inner circle and one in outer circle;
      Diagram of chlorine atom – three circles drawn, with 2 electrons in inner circle, eight electrons in middle circle and seven in outer circle;
      One mark for correct Li outer shell; one mark for correct Cl outer shell; one mark for correct inner shells for both Li and Cl. (3)
  c Chlorine gas is toxic. (1)
  d i Atoms of the same element (with same atomic/proton number) with different numbers of neutrons (different mass numbers) (1)
    ii Chlorine-37 has two more neutrons than chlorine-35 (1)

2 a

    i Prevents suck-back/cold water being sucked up (1)
      back into the hot test tube with would smash (1)
    ii Glowing splint/spill (1)
      relights (1)
  b $2NaNO_3(s) \rightarrow 2NaNO_2(s) + O_2(g)$ (2)
  c i 8.5 g of $NaNO_3$ is 8.5/85 mol = 0.1 mole from equation, 1 mole of $NaNO_3$ will give 1 mole of $NaNO_2$
      Mass of 1 mole of $NaNO_2$ is 69 so mass of 0.1 mole is $(0.1 \times 69) = 6.9$ g (3)
    ii Not all the $NaNO_3$ had decomposed or the sodium(v) nitrate was not pure. (1)

3 a 9.6 g (1)
  b i The simplest ratio of elements present in a compound. (1)

108

ii moles of K = 7.8/39
          = 0.2
    moles of Br = 16.0/80
          = 0.2
    moles of O = 9.6/16
          = 0.6
    Simplest ratio of K : Br : O = 1 : 1 : 3
    Empirical formula is $KBrO_3$ (4)

c   Relative formula (molecular) mass.   (1)

d   Close-packed, regular arrangement, particles touching   (1)
    Vibrating about fixed points   (1)

e i 12%   (1)
   ii moles of K = 29/39
          = 0.74
     moles of Br = 59/80
          = 0.74
     moles of O = 12/16
          = 0.75
     Simplest ratio of K : Br : O = 1 : 1 : 1
     Empirical formula is KBrO   (3)

3 Structure and bonding

▶ 3.1
1 It is made of non-metals.
2 KBr, Na_2O, MgO
3 Lithium atoms lose an electron to form a lithium ion that has a positive charge or Li^+; fluorine atoms gain an electron to form a fluoride ion that has a negative charge or F^-.

▶ 3.2
1 Sodium ions have a single positive charge – they are Na^+, and magnesium ions have a double positive charge: they are Mg^{2+} (chloride ions have a single negative charge and are Cl^-).

▶ 3.3
1 They have giant structures with strong electrostatic forces that hold the ions together and a lot of energy is needed to overcome the forces.
2 The ions can move freely and carry the charge.

▶ 3.4
1 Cl—Cl, H—Cl, H—S—H, O=O, O=C=O

▶ 3.5
1 The intermolecular forces are greater for larger molecules.
2 The bulb/lamp will light up if the liquid conducts electricity.
3 The molecules in ethanol have no overall charge.

▶ 3.6
1 Every atom is joined to several other atoms, many strong covalent bonds have to be broken and so it takes a large amount of energy to melt the giant structure.
2 Similarities: forms of carbon; giant covalent structures or covalent bonding. Differences: carbon atoms in diamond are bonded to four other carbon atoms, only to three other atoms in graphite; diamond is three-dimensional, graphite two-dimensional; diamond is hard, graphite is slippery/soft; diamond is transparent, graphite is grey/opaque; graphite is a good conductor of heat/electricity, diamond is a poor conductor; graphite has delocalised electrons, diamond does not; graphite has intermolecular forces, diamond does not.
3 Similarities: forms of carbon, hexagonal rings of atoms. Differences: graphite is a giant structure, fullerenes are molecules; graphite is two dimensional, fullerenes are three-dimensional/cage-like; graphite forms large particles, many fullerenes are nano-sized.

▶ 3.7
1 A very small particle that is a few nanometres in size, or made of a few hundreds of atoms.
2 Its effects on people and the environment should be researched/tested (to ensure it is safe to use). Carry out research/checks on the effects of the nanoparticles on human health.

Answers to end of Chapter 3 questions

1 a Outer electrons (electrons in the highest occupied energy level or outer shell).
  b They are transferred or metal atoms lose electrons and non-metal atoms gain electrons.
  c They are shared. For each covalent bond one pair of electrons is shared.

2 a They lose their one outer electron (one electron in the highest occupied energy level or outer shell).
  b They gain one electron so their highest energy level (outer shell) has eight electrons or so they have the structure of a noble gas.
3 LiCl, Na_2O, CaF_2, $Mg(OH)_2$, Na_2SO_4, $Ca(NO_3)_2$
4 Central C with 4 shared pairs of electrons (o x) around it and H outside each of the pairs of electrons.
5 F—F, O=O, H—Br, H—O—H, N with three lines, each to an H.
6 Diagram of a potassium atom showing one electron, fluorine atom with seven electrons, potassium ion with no electrons and positive charge, fluoride ion with eight electrons and a negative charge.
7 Forms of carbon, with large molecules, based on hexagonal rings of carbon atoms, often cage-like structures, can be nano-sized, have many useful applications.
8 It has a giant ionic structure with strong electrostatic forces/bonds that hold the oppositely charged ions firmly in position and that need a lot of energy to overcome/break them.
9 They are made of small molecules or covalent bonds act only between the atoms within a molecule.
10 The ions cannot move in the solid, but become free to move in the molten liquid or in solution.
11 There are delocalised electrons in graphite or one electron from each carbon atom is delocalised; the delocalised electrons carry the electrical charge.
12 Forces between molecules (that are much weaker than covalent bonds within the molecules).

4 Air and water

▶ 4.1
1 78% nitrogen (almost 80%), and 21% oxygen (just over 20%)
2 Air is a mixture of different substances that have different boiling points.

▶ 4.2
1 calcium + oxygen → calcium oxide
   2Ca   + O_2 →   2CaO
2 Purple, indicating strongly alkaline solution.
3 a Oxides that can behave like acidic oxides or basic oxides.
  b Acidic oxide – a non-metal oxide, such as carbon dioxide, sulfur dioxide. Basic oxide – a metal oxide, such as sodium oxide, magnesium oxide. Amphoteric oxide – e.g. aluminium oxide.

▶ 4.3
1 Sedimentation and/or filtration to remove solids, killing microbes (disinfecting/sterilising) using chlorine (or other methods, e.g. ozone, ultraviolet).
2 It reduces tooth decay but people have no choice/large doses can/might cause health problems.

▶ 4.4
1 To absorb water vapour from the air.
2 To compare the effectiveness of the different methods of protection against rust with no protection.

Answers to end of Chapter 4 questions

1 Four from: nitrogen, oxygen, water vapour, carbon dioxide, argon, any other named noble gas.
2 a To separate the air into individual gases, to produce (liquid) nitrogen and oxygen (also argon), which have commercial uses or are raw materials.
  b To separate the elements nitrogen, oxygen and argon, air is cooled to –200 °C, so that the gases become liquids. The liquid mixture is then put into a fractional distillation column that is colder at the bottom than the top. Nitrogen is collected from the top of the column as a gas and oxygen from the bottom as a liquid. Argon can be collected from the middle or with oxygen from the bottom of the column.
3 a iron + oxygen → iron(III) oxide
     4Fe(s) + $3O_2$(g) → $2Fe_2O_3$(s)
  b oxidation/redox/combustion
4 An alkali is a base which is soluble in water.
5 Magnesium oxide – basic; sodium oxide – basic; sulfur dioxide – acidic; hydrogen oxide – neutral; carbon dioxide – acidic; aluminium oxide – amphoteric
6 Potassium hydroxide
7 Insoluble solids
8 To kill microbes/bacteria
9 Prevent tooth decay/improve dental health
10 Both air (oxygen) and water
11 a The more reactive zinc reacts with oxygen and water rather than the less reactive iron.
   b Sacrificial protection

5 The periodic table

⟫ 5.1

1 They have the same number of electrons in the highest occupied energy level or outer shell.

2 Because their electronic structures are very stable.

⟫ 5.2

1 Potassium; lilac

2 They react with water to produce hydrogen gas and a metal hydroxide that is an alkali.

3 Potassium bromide, KBr

⟫ 5.3

1 They are strong, hard, react only slowly (or not at all) with oxygen/air and water (at ordinary temperatures).

2 Transition elements have higher melting points, stronger, harder, denser, less reactive (with oxygen and water), ions have different charges, coloured compounds, catalysts.

⟫ 5.4

1 They have small molecules (made of pairs of atoms).

2 Add chlorine (water) to a solution of potassium bromide (or other soluble bromide), bromine will be displaced.

⟫ 5.5

1 Going down a group, there are more occupied energy levels and the atoms get larger. As the atoms get larger, the electrons in the highest occupied energy level (outer shell) are further from the nucleus and so are less strongly attracted by the nucleus.

2 Lithium atoms are smaller than sodium atoms, they have fewer occupied energy levels (Li 2,1; Na 2,8,1), their outer electron is more strongly attracted by the nucleus, and so is less easily lost when they react (to form a positive ion).

Answers to end of Chapter 5 questions

1 The elements are arranged in order of atomic number.

2 The noble gases.

3 They have the same number of electrons in the highest occupied energy level or outer shell (same number of outer electrons).

4 a lithium + water → lithium hydroxide + hydrogen

  b Three from: lithium floats, moves around the surface, gradually disappears, bubbles (of gas) or fizzes.

  c Add (universal) indicator, goes purple or blue (or correct alkaline colour for named indicator).

  d Sodium reacts faster or melts (lithium does not melt).

5 Physical: (three from) high melting point (and/or boiling point), hard, strong, high density, malleable, ductile, good conductor (of heat and electricity), can be made into alloys. Chemical: (three from) unreactive or reacts slowly with oxygen (air) and/or water, forms positive ions/ionic compounds, forms ions with different charges, coloured compounds, catalyst.

6 They increase.

7 NaBr; colourless or white, crystals or solid; dissolves in water, forms a colourless solution.

8 Covalently bonded, small molecules (has weak forces between its molecules).

9 a From colourless to orange/yellow/brown.

  b chlorine + potassium bromide → potassium chloride + bromine

  c $Cl_2 + 2KBr \rightarrow 2KCl + Br_2$

10 $2Fe + 3Cl_2 \rightarrow 2FeCl_3$

11 a A sodium atom has more occupied energy levels/shells, so its outer electron is further from and less strongly held by the nucleus, and so can be more easily lost when it reacts.

  b A fluorine atom has fewer occupied energy levels/shells, so its nucleus has a greater attraction for electrons in the highest occupied energy level/outer shell, so it attracts electrons more readily when it reacts.

Answers to Examination-style questions

1 a i Two fluorine atoms with electrons arranged with two in the inner shell and seven in the outer shell. (1)

    The outer shells overlap with a pair of electrons shared. (1)

  ii Covalent (1)

  b i Magnesium electrons arranged as two in inner shell, eight in outer shell. (1)

    Fluorine electrons arranged as two in inner shell, eight in outer shell. (1)

  ii Neon (1)

  iii Mg^{2+} (1)

    F^- (1)

  iv MgF_2 (1)

  v Giant ionic (1)

  c 1 mark for each of:

    in magnesium fluoride there are strong (electrostatic) forces of attraction;

    between oppositely charged ions that act in all directions;

    so it takes a lot of energy to separate the ions/break down the giant lattice;

    whereas fluorine is made up of simple molecules;

    with weak forces of attraction between individual molecules. (5)

  d Fluorine is more reactive than chlorine (atomic number 17).

    i Nothing/no reaction would be observed (1)

      as chlorine is less reactive than fluorine so cannot displace the fluoride ion from its solution (1)

    ii bromine water + potassium iodide solution → potassium bromide + iodine (1)

    iii Displacement (1)

    iv 1 mark for each of:

      Chlorine and fluorine both react by gaining one electron into their outer shell/highest energy level;

      chlorine atoms are larger the fluorine atoms;

      so the outer shell of chlorine is further from the attractive force of the nucleus;

      Which means that the extra electron gained into that shell is not attracted as strongly as an extra electron gained into a fluorine atom. (4)

  e i To kill bacteria/microbes (1)

    ii To help prevent tooth decay (1)

    iii E.g. people have no choice in the matter /some health concerns caused by large doses of fluoride (1)

2 a A substance made up of only one type of atom. (1)

  b Alkali metals (1)

  c i Lithium bromide (1)

    ii LiBr (1)

      Li^+ (1)

      Br^- (1)

    iii

Colour of compound	Solubility of compound in water (soluble or insoluble?)	Melting point of compound (high or low?)
white	soluble	high

    (2 marks; 1 mark for colour; 1 mark for both solubility and melting point correct)

3 a i Sodium hydroxide (1)

    ii Hydrogen (1)

    iii A lighted splint ignites the gas with a (squeaky) pop

    iv $2Na(s) + 2H_2O(l) \rightarrow 2NaOH(aq) + H_2(g)$

      allow Na(l) (3)

  c 1 mark for each:

    Sodium and potassium react by losing their outer shell electron;

    A potassium atom has more occupied energy levels/shells or is larger than sodium atom;

    so its outer electron is further from and less strongly held by the nucleus;

    and so can be more easily lost when it reacts. (4)

6 Acids, bases and salts

⟫ 6.1

1 Hydrogen ions, $H^+(aq)$

2 A soluble *base* or a substance that produces hydroxide ions in solution, $OH^-(aq)$.

3 Universal indicator or full-range indicators.

⟫ 6.2

1 Any metal that is more reactive than hydrogen, but less reactive than calcium, e.g. lead, tin, iron, aluminium, magnesium.

2 To use up all of the acid or to neutralise all of the acid

⟫ 6.3

1 Water, H_2O

2 To wash away any solutions of unreacted reactants and the soluble product, potassium nitrate, which would crystallise out and contaminate the sample of lead iodide when dried.

3 Zinc carbonate would be produced as a precipitate or solid, sodium sulfate would remain in the solution.

6.4

1 Carbonates give off carbon dioxide gas when they react with dilute acids.
2 magnesium + hydrochloric → magnesium + carbon + water
  carbonate   acid   chloride   dioxide
  $MgCO_3(s)$ + $2HCl(aq)$ → $MgCl_2(aq)$ + $CO_2(g)$ + $H_2O(l)$
3 Zinc oxide (ZnO) and carbon dioxide (CO_2)

6.5

1 A pipette measures a fixed volume, has a single graduation, and has no tap; a burette measures different volumes, has graduations, has a tap.
2 To show when the end point is reached or when the reaction is complete or when the acid and alkali have reacted exactly.

6.6

1 $12 g/dm^3$, $0.5 mol/dm^3$
2 $0.17 mol/dm^3$

Answers to end of Chapter 6 questions

1 a An alkali
  b Neutralisation
  c The reaction shows no visible change and the indicator will show when the pH is 7.
  d nitric acid + sodium hydroxide → sodium nitrate + water
2 Add zinc oxide, a little at a time, to dilute sulfuric acid, until there is an excess, filter off the excess, evaporate some of the water, leave to cool and crystallise.
3 Mix the two solutions, filter the mixture or leave to settle and decant or centrifuge and decant to separate the solid (precipitate). Then wash with distilled water and dry.
4 Breaking down of a compound by heating.
5 Calcium oxide and carbon dioxide.
6 Calcium carbonate is formed and is insoluble.
  calcium   + carbon → calcium   + water
  hydroxide   dioxide   carbonate
  or $Ca(OH)_2$ + CO_2 → $CaCO_3$ + H_2O
7 Acids react with calcium carbonate producing carbon dioxide and a salt. The salt dissolves in water and so the amount of limestone decreases or is worn away.
8 Calcium hydroxide reacts with acids, because calcium hydroxide is an alkali, and the reaction is neutralisation (the pH of the soil increases, which is better for growing crops).
9 $K_2CO_3 + 2HCl → 2KCl + H_2O + CO_2$
10 $0.05 mol/dm^3$

7 Metals

7.1

1 Hydrogen (H_2)
2 a E.g. concentration of the acid, surface area/size of the piece(s) of metal, temperature
  b It is difficult to get samples of different metals with the same surface area.

7.2

1 zinc + copper(II) sulfate → zinc sulfate + copper
  $Zn(s)$ + $CuSO_4(aq)$ → $ZnSO_4(aq)$ + $Cu(s)$
2 magnesium, carbon, iron, hydrogen, copper
3 magnesium atoms are oxidised, copper(II) ions are reduced.

7.3

1 Rock from which metal can be extracted economically.
2 a Two metals from those below carbon in the reactivity series, e.g. zinc, iron, tin, lead, copper.
  b Reduction

7.4

1 High-grade ores are limited or running out, to reduce environmental impacts.
2 Smelting, electrolysis, displacement

7.5

1 To save: the energy needed to extract it from its ore, resources, fossil fuels, land needed for mining and/or landfill, other **specified** environmental impact as extraction can cause pollution.
2 Copper in scrap metal has often been alloyed so is a mixture of metals.

7.6

1 In a giant structure, closely packed together in layers with a regular pattern.
2 Electrostatic forces between positive (metal) ions and delocalised electrons.

7.7

1 When stretched, the atoms slide into new positions without breaking apart.

2 They are harder than pure metals; they can be made/designed to have specific properties or special properties such as shape memory alloys.
3 Delocalised electrons move rapidly through the metal structure.

7.8

1 Strong, good conductors of heat and electricity, can be bent and hammered into shape.
2 Good conductor of electricity, can be made into wires, can be bent into shape, resistant to corrosion.
3 To make it harder.

7.9

1 It is brittle.
2 They are harder, can be made with specific properties, can be made to resist corrosion.

Answers to end of Chapter 7 questions

1 Ore
2 It is very unreactive or very low in the reactivity series.
3 Strong, good conductors of heat and electricity, can be bent and hammered into shape, can be drawn out into wires, sonorous.
4 Most pure metals are too soft for many uses, they need to be made harder by alloying (mixing with other elements).
5 Reduction.
  iron oxide + carbon → iron + carbon dioxide
6 Low-carbon steel or mild steel, easily shaped; high-carbon steel, hard; stainless steel, resists corrosion.
7 All steels contain iron and carbon, so are mixtures of a metal with at least one other element.
8 Three from: to save iron ore or reduce mining, to save energy or fossil fuels needed for extraction, to reduce waste going to land fill, to reduce imports of iron or iron ore
9 $CO_2 + C → 2CO$
  $2Fe_2O_3 + 3C → 4Fe + 3CO_2$
  $Fe_2O_3 + 3CO → 2Fe + 3CO_2$
10 Phytomining and bioleaching. Phytomining uses plants to absorb copper compounds from the ground. The plants are burned and produce ash. This can be smelted to produce copper or reacted with acid to produce a solution that can be electrolysed or to which iron can be added to produce copper. Bioleaching uses bacteria to produce a solution of copper compounds that can be electrolysed or to which iron can be added to produce copper.
11 The outer electrons in metal atoms delocalise, leaving a lattice of positive ions; the delocalised electrons strongly attract the positive ions and hold them in position. The delocalised electrons are free to drift around in the structure and can carry the electrical charge through the giant lattice, making metals good conductors of electricity.

8 Rates of reaction

8.1

1 Amount (of reactant or product) and time.
2 The gradient of the line at a given time gives the rate at that time.
3 The line would start at the origin, then curve upwards (positive slope) before levelling off.

8.2

1 Activation energy
2 Powders have greater surface area than large lumps of solid, and this increases the chance of collisions.
3 Temperature, concentration of acid, volume of acid, mass of calcium carbonate.

8.3

1 It increases the frequency of collisions as well as the energy of the particles.
2 It is difficult to judge exactly when the cross marked under the flask disappears from view.
3 Repeat each test at least three times and work out the mean of the timings with the least variation, discarding any anomalous readings.

8.4

1 It increases the frequency of collisions.
2 The frequency of collisions increases because there are more molecules in the same volume.
3 The higher the concentration, the faster the rate of reaction.

8.5

1 They remain chemically unchanged at the end of a reaction or they are not used up in the reaction.

2 a They reduce the energy needed and the time needed, and so reduce costs. They may reduce the amount of fossil fuel used and so conserve resources and reduce pollution.
b They may be toxic or expensive.
3 A bar chart (as the independent variable – the type of catalyst – is a categoric variable; see Experimental data analysis section).

Answers to end of Chapter 8 questions

1 Increase concentration of acid, increase temperature, use powdered zinc, use a catalyst.
2 The volume of gas; the loss in mass
3 From the gradient or slope of the line.
4 The minimum energy that particles must have for collisions to produce a reaction.
5 Fastest = iron filings, slowest = a block of iron.
6 A substance that increases the rate of reaction without being chemically changed itself at the end of the reaction.
7 Inverted measuring cylinder/burette to collect the gas over water or a gas syringe.
8 High temperature, high pressure, catalyst
9 Particles are closer together (more particles in the same volume), so collisions are more frequent (more collisions per second).
10 Particles collide more frequently, and with more energy so more collisions in a given time will have the activation energy (the minimum energy needed for a reaction to take place).

Answers to Examination-style questions

1 a The solution becomes cloudy (1)
 as solid sulfur forms in a precipitation reaction (1)
 and light can no longer pass through the solution (1)
b Add water to thiosulfate solution (1)
 measured in measuring cylinder/volume kept constant (1)
c temperature, volume of thiosulfate solution (2)
d i the time decreases (1)
ii The rate of reaction increases (1)
 as the concentration increases (1)
iii increase in concentration gives more particles in same volume; (1)
 so there are more collisions between particles per unit time/there is a greater chance of particles colliding; resulting in more frequent collisions that result in a reaction (3)
e Marks awarded for this answer will be determined by the Quality of Written Communication (QWC) as well as the standard of the scientific response.
 There is a clear and detailed scientific description of the plan with almost faultless spelling, punctuation and grammar. It is coherent and in an organised, logical sequence. It contains a range of appropriate and relevant specialist terms used accurately when describing how to set up a fair test. This plan could easily be followed by another person. (5–6)
 There is a clear description of the plan, which includes most of the apparatus needed, and an explanation of setting up a fair test. The plan could be followed by another person. There is an attempt at identifying some, but not necessarily all, of the apparatus and safety precautions needed. The use of specialist terms has been attempted, but not always applied accurately. (3–4)
 There is a brief description of the plan. The spelling, punctuation and grammar are very weak. The answer is poorly organised with almost no specialist terms and/or their use demonstrates a general lack of understanding of fair testing and collecting accurate data. (1–2)
 No relevant content. (0)
 Examples of chemistry points made in the response:
 Only temperature varied (thermometer used); Acid and thiosulfate solutions at same temperature when tested; Timing with stopclock/watch; Need for repeat readings; How to deal with repeat readings; Control variables kept constant e.g. concentration and volume of solutions (measuring cylinder); Details of how to heat the solutions e.g. Bunsen, tripod, gauze/water bath; Discuss how to move hot flask; How to follow course of reaction; Conical flask, cross marked on paper; Possible use light sensor and data logger to monitor reaction; Eye protection worn
2 a It contains enough zinc to make it worthwhile/economic to extract. (1)
b It contains more than one element/zinc and sulfur (1)
c i zinc sulfide + oxygen → zinc oxide + sulfur dioxide (1)
ii $2ZnS(s) + 3O_2(g) \rightarrow 2ZnO(s) + 2SO_2(g)$ (3)

d i zinc oxide + carbon monoxide → zinc + carbon dioxide (1)
ii The zinc ions (Zn^{2+}) gain two electrons (1)
 and change to zinc atoms (Zn) (1)
 as they are reduced by the carbon monoxide (1)

9 Crude oil and fuels

▶ 9.1
1 Liquids with different boiling ranges separated from a mixture of liquids (crude oil).
2 It has the general formula C_nH_{2n+2}, it is a saturated compound, it has only single carbon—carbon bonds.
3 C_4H_{10}

▶ 9.2
1 Different hydrocarbons have different boiling points (so they condense at different temperatures at different levels).
2 Medium-high boiling point (about 250 °C), quite viscous/oily/thick liquid, not very flammable, burns with quite a smoky flame.

▶ 9.3
Practical questions
1 a Limewater turns cloudy, showing carbon dioxide gas is given off.
b Condensation forms; blue cobalt chloride paper turns pink; water is present
2 ethane + oxygen → carbon dioxide + water
3 carbon monoxide, carbon, unburnt hydrocarbon, water
4 Acid rain

▶ 9.4
1 Biodiesel, ethanol
2 Advantage: no pollution or only product is water or can be made from water. Disadvantage: difficult to store or production requires large amount of energy.

Answers to end of Chapter 9 questions

1 To make useful fuels/products
2 Carbon dioxide and water
3 Ignite/burn more easily, thin/runny liquids, burn with clean flame/little smoke
4 Two from: biodiesel, ethanol, hydrogen
5 Solid soot/carbon and unburnt fuel/ hydrocarbons, produced by incomplete combustion.
6 a The fuel contains sulfur (compounds); these oxidise/burn to produce sulfur dioxide.
b The sulfur can be removed from the fuel before it is burned e.g. as in petrol, and sulfur dioxide gas can be removed from waste gases released when the fuel burns e.g. by scrubbers inside chimneys at fossil fuel power stations.
7 Poisonous gas carbon monoxide may be produced in limited supply of air.
8 The carbon was locked-up in fossil fuels; increases carbon dioxide in the atmosphere; carbon dioxide is a greenhouse gas; may cause global warming.
9 12 H joined to 5C, all single bonds, each C with four single bonds ($CH_3CH_2CH_2CH_2CH_3$). Four from: alkane, saturated, hydrocarbon, general formula C_nH_{2n+2}, has only single bonds, burns to produce carbon dioxide and water.
10 Crude oil vapour enters column, vapour rises, until boiling point of compound is reached, compound condenses (at that level), collected as liquid (from that level), high boiling fractions collected at bottom of column, low boiling fractions collected at top.
11 $C_2H_6O + 3O_2 \rightarrow 2CO_2 + 3H_2O$
12 $2H_2 + O_2 \rightarrow 2H_2O$, only product is water, no pollution, no carbon dioxide produced, can be made from water, electricity needed can be made using renewable energy source.

10 Other products from crude oil

▶ 10.1
1 One from: to make fuels that are more useful or for which there is more demand, large hydrocarbons do not burn easily or are less in demand.
2 Three from: are unsaturated, have a double bond, have a different general formula, have fewer hydrogen atoms than the corresponding alkane, are more reactive, react with or decolourise bromine water.

▶ 10.2
1 From many small molecules or monomers that react or join together or polymerise to make a very large or very long molecule.

2 Thousands or a very large number.

3 Alkenes are more reactive or are unsaturated or have a double bond, alkanes are unreactive or saturated or do not have a double bond.

10.3

1 They are made using different reaction conditions; they have different structures or differently shaped molecules.

2 Thermosoftening polymers have no cross-links or no covalent bonds between the polymer chains, thermosetting polymers have cross-links.

3 There are weak intermolecular forces between the chains (which are overcome by heating).

10.4

1 A type of smart polymer or a polymer that can change to its original shape when temperature or other conditions change.

2 Two medical uses: e.g. dental fillings, removable sticking plasters, wound dressings, stitches; and two non-medical uses: e.g. packaging, waterproof fabrics, containers, bottles, clothing, fibres for duvets, water-holding composts

10.5

1 The litter would be decomposed by microorganisms when in contact with soil, and so it would not remain in the environment.

2 It can be added to plastics made from non-biodegradable polymers so they break down into small pieces when microorganisms in the soil digest the cornstarch; it can also be used itself to make biodegradable plastic.

Answers to end of Chapter 10 questions

1 Two from: to make alkenes, to make alkanes with smaller molecules, to make fuels that are more useful or for which there is more demand, large hydrocarbons do not burn easily or are less in demand, to make polymers (from alkenes).

2 By heating a mixture of hydrocarbon vapours and steam to a very high temperature, by passing hydrocarbon vapours over a hot catalyst.

3 Alkanes: C_5H_{12}, C_4H_{10}, C_6H_{14} Alkenes: C_3H_6, C_4H_8

4 A polymer has very large molecules made from many small molecules called monomers joined together by a polymerisation reaction.

5 Example of use of smart polymer, e.g. shape-memory polymer used for stitching wounds.

6 Can be broken down by microorganisms.

7 Three from e.g. use biodegradable polymers, recycle, use plastics with cornstarch mixed in, use light-sensitive polymers, collect litter/rubbish for proper disposal.

8 By fermentation of sugar with yeast, advantages: renewable source, room temperature, disadvantages: dilute solution of ethanol, needs to be distilled to make pure ethanol, slow, batch process; by hydration of ethene with steam and a catalyst, advantages: pure ethanol produced, continuous process, fast, disadvantages: non-renewable source, high temperature needed.

9 a

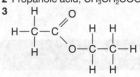

NB CH_3 can be shown as

$$H-\overset{\displaystyle H}{\underset{\displaystyle H}{C}}-H$$

b $C_2H_4 + H_2O \rightleftharpoons CH_3CH_2OH$ (or C_2H_5OH)

10 C_2H_4

11 They do not soften/melt when they get hot, they are good insulators (of heat), they can be moulded into shape but then are rigid/hard.

12 Different monomers change the structure of the polymer chains or the polymer chains have different shapes/structures.

11 Alcohols, carboxylic acids and esters

11.1

1 methane, ethane and propane

2 $CH_3CH_2CH_2OH$

3

$$H-C\overset{\displaystyle \nearrow O}{\underset{\displaystyle \searrow O-H}{}}$$

Methanoic acid

11.2

1 It is a solvent (it mixes with water, it evaporates easily).

2 One of: apply a flame – ethanol burns in air: add sodium – ethanol reacts more slowly (also sinks in ethanol): add (acidified) potassium dichromate (or other oxidising agent) and heat – colour change or smell of vinegar

11.3

1 They produce $H^+(aq)$, hydrogen ions in aqueous solutions.

2 They have distinctive smells/tastes that are fruity/ pleasant.

3 $CH_3CH_2COOH(aq) \rightleftharpoons CH_3CH_2COO^-(aq) + H^+(aq)$

Answers to end of Chapter 11 questions

1 Methanol, ethanol and propanol, CH_3OH, CH_3CH_2OH, $CH_3CH_2CH_2OH$

2 Propanoic acid, CH_3CH_2COOH

3

Ethyl ethanoate

4 It reacts, fizzes/effervesces, produces hydrogen (slower than with water, sodium sinks)

5 Microbes in the air, caused oxidation of ethanol, produced ethanoic acid.

6 Reacts with carbonates to produce carbon dioxide (and a salt and water) or reacts with metals to produce hydrogen and a salt, or reacts with bases/ alkalis to produce a salt and water.

7 Ethyl ethanoate, (sulfuric) acid catalyst, heat the mixture.

8 It is an ester and so has a fruity smell/flavour.

9 ethanoic acid + sodium hydroxide → sodium ethanoate + water
$CH_3COOH(aq) + NaOH(aq) → CH_3COONa(aq) + H_2O(l)$

10 $2CH_3CH_2CH_2OH + 9O_2 → 6CO_2 + 8H_2O$
or $CH_3CH_2CH_2OH + 4.5O_2 → 3CO_2 + 4H_2O$
Test with universal indicator or pH meter/probe, ethanoic acid has higher pH: or add a metal, such as magnesium (not sodium as its reaction with dilute hydrochloric acid is too violent) or carbonate, ethanoic acid reacts (gives off a gas) more slowly.

11 Hydrochloric acid ionises completely in aqueous solutions:
$$HCl(aq) → H^+(aq) + Cl^-(aq)$$
Whereas ethanoic acid is only partially ionised in aqueous solution. The reaction is reversible:
$$CH_3COOH(aq) \rightleftharpoons CH_3COO^-(aq) + H^+(aq)$$
So for a given concentration ethanoic acid will not produce as high a concentration of $H^+(aq)$ ions as hydrochloric acid.

Answers to Examination-style questions

1 a i A compound made up of hydrogen and carbon only (1)

  ii A mixture of hydrocarbons with similar boiling points (1)

  iii Fractional distillation (1)

 b i Cracking (1)

  ii $C_{10}H_{22} → C_8H_{18} + C_2H_4$ (1)

  iii Fuels (1)

  iv A substance that speeds up a reaction but remains chemically unchanged itself at the end of the reaction. (1)

  v To increase the rate of reaction/effectiveness of the catalyst (1)
   by increasing its surface area. (1)

  vi 1 mark for each:
   • particles gain more energy the higher the temperature is;
   • so travel at a greater average speed;
   • so there are more frequent collisions between particles;
   • and a greater proportion of the collisions have sufficient energy to react/have the activation energy (4)

 c i Polymerisation (1)

  ii

   Ethene (2)

  iii Ethene contains a double bond whereas ethane has only single bonds (1)

 d Add yellow/orange bromine water (1)
   Ethene decolourises the bromine water/turns colourless (1)
   Ethane has no effect on the bromine water – it stays yellow/orange (1)

2 a

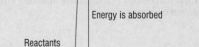

Ethanoic acid (1)

b i bubbles of gas/effervesces/fizzing (1)
ii One mark each for sodium ethanoate, carbon dioxide, water (3)
c i Hydrogen (1)
ii Test with lighted splint/spill (1)
burns with (results in) a (squeaky) pop (1)
d i Esters (1)
ii Ethyl ethanoate (1)
iii Ethanol (1)
iv Water (1)
v Sulfuric acid (1)
vi Perfume/flavourings (1)

12 Energy changes in chemical reactions

▶ 12.1
1 It transfers energy to the surroundings or heats the surroundings.
2 Either it cools the surroundings or it needs to be heated to keep it going.
3 Reduce heat loss e.g. by using a lid on the Styrofoam cup or use a temperature sensor and data logger to record the temperatures.

▶ 12.2
1 One advantage e.g. less waste, less materials/ resources used; one disadvantage e.g. has to be heated or needs energy so it can be used again, slower reaction, smaller temperature rise.
2 One advantage e.g. can be used anywhere, can be stored easily (ice needs to be made and/or stored in special equipment); one disadvantage e.g. can only be used once, more waste, possibly more hazardous than ice.

▶ 12.3
1 It is an endothermic reaction.
2 It is an exothermic reaction.

▶ 12.4
1 36 400 J or 36.4 kJ
2 Fuel B (A releases 2620.8 kJ/mol and B releases 4058.4 kJ/mol)

▶ 12.5
1 7560 J or = 7.56 kJ
2 142.8 kJ/mol of iron

▶ 12.6
1

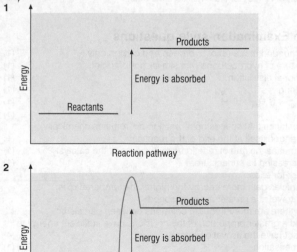

2

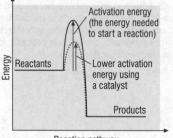

3

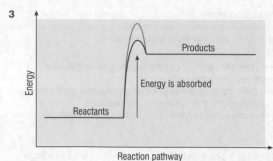

▶ 12.7
1 Bonds broken: $(2 \times C\!-\!C) + (8 \times C\!-\!H) + (5 \times O\!=\!O)$, energy needed = +6488 kJ
Bonds made, energy released: $6 \times C\!=\!O + 8 \times H\!-\!O = -8542$ kJ
Energy change of reaction = −2054 kJ/mol

Answers to end of Chapter 12 questions

1 The minimum energy needed for a reaction to take place.
2 Any two e.g. neutralisation, displacement, combustion (respiration).
3 Because it is an endothermic reaction.
4 Energy losses or it is not only the water that is heated.
5 The energy level of the reactants is below the level of the products.
6

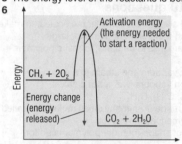

7 Energy released = 12 600 J or 12.6 kJ (or 25.2 kJ/g)
8 −75.6 kJ/mol
9 −58.8 kJ/mol
10

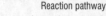

11 −542 kJ/mol
12 −1318 kJ/mol

13 The production of ammonia

▶ 13.1
1 When the rates of the forward and reverse reactions of a reversible reaction are equal or when the amounts of reactants and products in a reversible reaction are constant.
2 So that more of the reactants react or so more SO_3 is produced.

▶ 13.2
1 An increase in pressure
2 A decrease in temperature

▶ 13.3
1 nitrogen + hydrogen $\rightleftharpoons$ ammonia
2 Unreacted gases are recycled.

▶ 13.4
1 More energy is needed and stronger reaction vessels and pipes are needed which both cost more.
2 The reaction would be too slow (rate decreased and catalyst will not work).

Answers to end of Chapter 13 questions

1 A reversible reaction
2 Eventually the rate of the forward reaction will be the same as the rate of the reverse reaction so overall there will be no change in the concentration of reactants or products once this state of equilibrium has been reached.
3 The position of equilibrium will shift to the left to make more chlorine.
4 The position of equilibrium will shift to the right to favour the side with the least number of gas molecules (chlorine is the only gas in the equilibrium mixture).
5 Increase the temperature.
6 a Air (nitrogen), natural gas (hydrogen)
  b About 200 atmospheres pressure, about 450°C, iron catalyst.
  c The gases are cooled (as they leave the reactor) and ammonia condenses (liquefies) but nitrogen and hydrogen remain as gases.
7 Although a high temperature favours the reactants (nitrogen and hydrogen) i.e. the higher the temperature, the lower the yield of ammonia, a reasonably high temperature of 450°C must be used in industry to increase the rate of reaction.

14 Electrolysis

▶ 14.1
1 They must be melted or dissolved in water.
2 a Orange/brown vapour
  b Molten lead
3 a Chlorine
  b Zinc

▶ 14.2
1 Reduction or positive sodium ions gain electrons.
2 $2Cl^- \rightarrow Cl_2 + 2e^-$
3 a Oxygen
  b Copper

▶ 14.3
1 To lower the melting temperature.
2 Aluminium and oxygen.

▶ 14.4
1 The solution contains hydrogen ions which are discharged in preference to sodium ions because sodium is more reactive than hydrogen.
2 a chlorine at anode – bleaches damp blue litmus paper; hydrogen at cathode – burns with a squeaky pop with a lighted splint.
  b UI turns purple indicating a strongly alkaline solution (of sodium hydroxide).
3 Its (three) products have many uses or can be used in many ways.

▶ 14.5
1 To make them look attractive, to protect the metal from corrosion, to reduce the cost (of making the items from pure silver).
2 Nickel is plated onto the bare copper metal.
3 Pass electricity through a cell with the item of jewellery as the negative electrode, the positive electrode made of silver and containing a solution of a silver salt (e.g. silver nitrate solution) (as the electrolyte).

Answers to end of Chapter 14 questions

1 a Anode – chlorine; cathode – calcium
  b Anode – iodine; cathode – lithium
  c Anode – bromine; cathode – lead
2 a Anode – chlorine; cathode – copper
  b Anode – bromine; cathode – hydrogen
3 Hydrogen, chlorine and sodium hydroxide. A use for each, e.g. hydrogen: to make hydrochloric acid, margarine manufacture, fuel; chlorine: to make bleach, plastics; sodium hydroxide: to make soap, paper, as a cleaning agent (ovens/drains).
4 a It needs: large amounts of electricity, high temperature to melt the aluminium oxide.
  b To lower the melting/operating temperature (of the electrolyte).
5 a $Al^{3+} + 3e^- \rightarrow Al$
  b $2O^{2-} \rightarrow O_2 + 4e^-$
6 At the negative electrode: sodium ions gain electrons, are reduced, to sodium atoms/metal.
  At the positive electrode: chloride ions lose electrons, are oxidised, to chlorine atoms, which form chlorine molecules/gas.
7 At the cathode (negative electrode): $2H^+ + 2e^- \rightarrow H_2$
  At the anode (positive electrode): $2Cl^- \rightarrow Cl_2 + 2e^-$

8 Less expensive than pure gold, to improve appearance, so they do not corrode (or cause allergic reactions).
9 a Anode: $Ni \rightarrow Ni^{2+} + 2e^-$
  b Cathode: $Ni^{2+} + 2e^- \rightarrow Ni$

15 Analysis

▶ 15.1
1 Lithium (Li^+) and calcium (Ca^{2+})
2 Calcium (Ca^{2+}) and magnesium (Mg^{2+})

▶ 15.2
1 Carbon dioxide
2 Hydrochloric acid contains chloride ions (Cl^-) and sulfuric acid contains sulfate ions (SO_4^{2-}) which both give precipitates with silver nitrate solution.

▶ 15.3
1 a) sulfur; b) copper sulfate solution
2 Condenser

▶ 15.4
1 Paper chromatography
2 How many and what colour dyes are contained in each food colouring.

▶ 15.5
1 To separate the compounds (in the mixture).
2 From the molecular ion peak or the peak with the largest mass (furthest to the right in the mass spectrum).

Answers to end of Chapter 15 questions

1 $Fe^{3+}(aq) + 3OH^-(aq) \rightarrow Fe(OH)_3(s)$
2 Green
3 A white precipitate formed when dilute hydrochloric acid and then barium chloride solution is added.
4 Fe^{2+}/iron(II) ions and SO_4^{2-}/sulfate ions
5 Potassium iodide (KI)
6 Copper(II) carbonate ($CuCO_3$)
7 Food colourings/additives
8 0.25
9 The relative formula (molecular) mass.
10 Crystallisation/evaporation
11 Add water, stir, filter, wash the sand left on the filter paper with distilled water, dry in warm oven.
12 Boil the seawater in distillation apparatus; the water boils and leaves the flask as a vapour which enters the condenser. There it is cooled down and the vapour condenses to form pure liquid water that drips from the end of the condenser to be collected.

Answers to Examination-style questions

1 a i Zero/0/(amps)/no reading   (1)
    ii The ions are fixed in position in the solid;   (1)
       so cannot move to the electrodes   (1)
    iii A Bunsen burner cannot heat sodium chloride to a high enough temperature to melt it;
        so electrolysis is not possible in a school laboratory;
        If it was possible, the products are both hazardous;
        Molten sodium is very reactive/flammable
        Chlorine gas is toxic   (5)
  b i OH^- (1)
    ii H_2 (1)
    iii $2e^-$ (1)
    iv Water   (1)
    v Chlorine   (1)
    vi Hydrogen   (1)
  c Carbon/graphite/platinum   (1)
  d Purple colour;
    Strongly alkaline solution
    Sodium hydroxide in solution
    As H^+ ions are removed at cathode, leaving excess hydroxide/OH^- ions   (4)
  e Marks awarded for this answer will be determined by the Quality of Written Communication (QWC) as well as the standard of the scientific response. There is a clear and detailed scientific description of the process of electroplating with the answer showing almost faultless spelling, punctuation and grammar. The explanation is coherent and in an organised, logical sequence. It contains a range of appropriate and relevant specialist terms used accurately, including half equations.   (5–6)

There is a scientific description of electroplating. There are some errors in spelling, punctuation and grammar. The explanation has some structure and organisation but the use of specialist terms is not always accurate. Some labels missing from diagram and no state symbols in half equations but one half equation is correct. (3–4)

There is a brief description of the results of electroplating. The spelling, punctuation and grammar are very weak. The answer is poorly organised with almost no specialist terms and/or their use demonstrating a general lack of understanding of their meaning. (1–2)

No relevant content. (0)

Examples of chemistry points made in the response:
Diagram of circuit with the key as the cathode, nickel rod as anode, a nickel salt electrolyte, power source; Half equations – at anode:
$Ni(s) \rightarrow Ni^{2+}(aq) + 2\,e^-$; at cathode: $Ni^{2+}(aq) + 2e^- \rightarrow Ni(s)$; Ni^{2+} ions move to the cathode through the electrolyte which contains nickel ions/is a nickel salt; Ni atoms lose two electrons; Ni atoms are oxidised; Ni^{2+} ions gain two electrons; Ni^{2+} ions are reduced; low current for more effective plating (6)

2 a i Na^+/sodium ions are present (1)
  ii SO_4^{2-}/sulfate ions are present (1)
  iii Na_2SO_4 (1)
 b i Magnesium bromide (1)
   Aluminium bromide (1)
  ii Add excess sodium hydroxide solution to the white precipitate formed in Test 3. (1)
   If it is magnesium bromide, the white precipitate remains. (1)
   If it is aluminium bromide, the white precipitate dissolves. (1)
 c i Any two from: quicker, more accurate, detect smaller quantities. (2)
  ii To separate the substances in a mixture. (1)
  iii Its relative formula mass is 46. (1)
   The pattern of peaks can be used to identify the substance. (1)
   By matching against patterns of known substances (in a database). (1)